Whitlam's Foreign Policy

Michael Easson

Connor Court Publishing

Copyright © 2023, Michael Easson

ALL RIGHTS RESERVED. This book contains material protected under International and Federal Copyright Laws and Treaties. Any unauthorised reprint or use of this material is prohibited. No part of this book may be reproduced or transmitted in any form or by any means, electronic or mechanical, including photocopying, recording, or by any information storage and retrieval system without express written permission from the publisher.

CONNOR COURT PUBLISHING PTY LTD
PO Box 7257
Redland Bay QLD 4165
sales@connorcourt.com
www.connorcourt.com

Front cover: Whitlam leaving Beijing in November 1973. National Archives of Australia

Back cover: Whitlam and Nixon at the White House, 30 July, 1973. Photograph from the Nixon Presidential Library.

ISBN: 9781922815491

Printed in Australia

To Mary, my favourite dewy-eyed Whitlamite

Contents

Introduction	7
Whitlam and Whitlamisn	9
Five Hallmarks	27
An Issue of Neutral Significance	54
Controversies	57
Iraqi Ba'ath Socialist Party Loan Affair	79
Assessment	82
Author's Postscript	90
Bibliography	95
Index	109

Introduction

On one view, Gough Whitlam was a passing flash, whose government was not around long enough to have had an appreciable impact on Australian foreign policy. On another, Whitlam's foreign policy changes were immense and long lasting. Gareth Evans, Australia's Minister for Foreign Affairs, 1988-96, was aligned to the former position when he summarised: "A meteorite, short and dramatic, rather than a star, stable and lasting" (Evans & Grant 1991: 26). But he later refreshed his thinking about Whitlam's influence and significance: "...[I]t is only with Whitlam... that one finds nationalism, internationalism, and activism all really flourishing, and giving distinct character..." (Evans 1997: 13). Graham Freudenberg, Whitlam's Boswell, speechwriter, intellectual collaborator, and Labor historian declared that Whitlam was pivotal to major shifts in national policy (Freudenberg 1993). In addition to being prime minister, Whitlam was Minister for Foreign Affairs from December 1972 to November 1973 and, following Senator Don Willesee's appointment on 6 November 1973, government spokesman on Foreign Affairs in the House of Representatives. Before becoming Foreign Affairs Minister Willesee's ministerial portfolios included "Minister assisting the Minister for Foreign Affairs" (Paul 1973b: 116). As principal architect of Australian foreign policy: "no prime minister before [Whitlam] had exercised such untrammelled power in this area" (Viviani 1997: 102).

This essay, necessarily briefly, discusses the promise, creativity, problems, and influence of Whitlam's foreign policy. By looking objectively at key policy challenges and decisions made by Whitlam in the context of his time, some lasting impacts of the challenges and decisions made are highlighted. The rest of this chapter divides into five sections: on Whitlam & Whitlamism, five hallmarks of policy initiative (China relations, Papua New Guinea independence, the ANZUS alliance, a settlement on the joint Australian-US defence bases, Indonesian relations); then a matter of minor significance – Whitlam's trips; then, areas of controversy – Vietnamese refugees, East Timor independence, recognition of the Baltic states, Middle East policy, and the attempted Iraqi Ba'ath party loan transaction in 1975; and, finally, an assessment.

Through such analysis, mature reflection on Australia's legacy in relation to its obligations to and treatment of our alliances, commitment to the region, and human rights, and an appreciation of the idealist and realist strands of Whitlam's approach to foreign policy, is possible.

WHITLAM AND WHITLAMISM

Dean Acheson (1893-1971), US Secretary of State, 1949-53, leading architect of the foreign policy architecture of the post-war world, marvellously summarised in his memoirs, *Present at the Creation*, the complex pressures in this field on an American President, making points applicable to any serious country's leader:

> The capacity for decision... does not produce, of itself, wise decisions. For that a President needs a better eye and more intuition and coordination than the best batters in the major leagues. If his score is not far better than theirs, he will be rated a failure. But the metaphor is inadequate; it leaves out the necessary creativity. A President is not merely coping with the deliveries of others. He is called upon to influence and move to some degree his own country and the world around it to a purpose that he envisions. The metaphor I have often used and find most enlightening is that of the gardener who must use the forces of life, growth and nature, to his purpose – suppressing some, selecting, encouraging, developing others. The central role of directing so great an effort of imagination, planning, and action cannot come, as some seem to imagine, from such spontaneous intuition among the hired hands as guides a flock of shorebirds in flight. It must come from the head gardener... (Acheson 1970: 731).

In the Australian context, Gough Whitlam was chief batsman, weed puller, and imagination driver.

In the memoir of his prime ministership, *The Whitlam Government 1972-1975* (1985), the 156-page chapter on "International Affairs" easily eclipses any other in length; the other 20 chapters having an average of 28 pages. Whitlam prioritised this area of responsibility above all others. As he explained:

> Foreign policy was one of my government's strongest and most successful areas of achievement ... in foreign as in domestic matters, the programs which we most promptly and effectively implemented were those we had most thoroughly thought out and thought through and most fully established in public acceptance; and because of the special intensity of the public debate... (Whitlam 1985: 25).

Freudenberg argued that of all government agencies, the Department of Foreign Affairs was best prepared to handle the transition to government by Labor in December 1972: "I instance the fact that the oft-quoted statement of intent which Whitlam made at his first Prime Ministerial press conference on 5 December 1972 was submitted unsought by Dick Woolcott... and accepted by Whitlam without amendment" (Freudenberg 1993: 201). The career of Richard ("Dick") Woolcott (1927-2023) included periods as Ambassador to Indonesia, 1975-1978, and as head of the Department of Foreign Affairs and Trade, 1988-1992. His words, declared by Whitlam, were: "A more independent Australian stance in international affairs, an Australia which will be less militarily oriented and not open to suggestions of racism" (Bilney 2013: 278; Fitzgerald 2015: 94; Woolcott 2003: 112). Those themes were core to "Whitlamism" in foreign policy – the values, ideals, principles that underpinned policy promise – as distinct from the achievements, shortcomings, and record of the person.

Freudenberg quotes Whitlam's speech at the ALP launch of his election campaign in November 1972 as encapsulating key priorities:

> A nation's foreign policy depends on striking a wise, proper and prudent balance between commitment and power. Labor will have four commitments commensurate to our power and resources:
>
> > First – to our own national security;
> >
> > Secondly – to a secure, united, and friendly Papua New Guinea:
> >
> > Thirdly – to achieve closer relations with our nearest and largest neighbour, Indonesia;
> >
> > Fourthly – to promote the peace and prosperity of our neighbourhood. (Freudenberg 1993: 208).

Nancy Viviani acutely addressed the question of how a distinct Labor foreign policy tradition might be described – the characteristic mix of nationalism, internationalism, principle, pragmatism, and activism. She assessed Whitlam's contribution in forging it. This is not to suggest that every time a change of government occurs, a revolution in thinking and policies follows. Indeed, during and since World War II, all Australian governments have based their foreign policies in relation to the US alliance, regional engagement, and the "rules-based order." Whitlam explained that much of the advice his government received from the Department of Foreign Affairs and other government agencies was "the same which was available to the previous government. The continuity of that advice provides a valuable element in the continuity of Australia's foreign policy" (Whitlam 1973b: 335). But there were differences in outlook, perceptions of the world, strategies, and priorities. Whitlam was entrepreneurial and bold in developing new relationships. He scared the horses, insisting: "... the change is real and deep because what has altered is the perception and interpretation of those interests, obligations, and friendships by the elected government" (Whitlam 1973b: 1). Viviani surmises: "What is distinct in the values is, of course, the idea that Labor's concern for equality and social justice does not end at national borders." (Viviani 1997: 99). She sees three themes that predominate: nationalism, regionalism, international citizenship.

Distinct policy positions were taken early on: recognition of China; bringing home the last troops from Vietnam; acceleration of PNG's independence; burial of the White Australia policy; and bringing France before the International Court of Justice (ICJ) over nuclear testing, as well as the commitment to process (international treaties) (Evans 1997: 13). After the majority judgement by the ICJ on 20 December 1974, Whitlam explained: "...[T]he Australian Government does not regard recourse to the World Court as an unfriendly act in any way; it is simply an appropriate means for settling disputes in a civilised, reasoned way" (Whitlam 1975b: 449). "In 1974 Australia supported resolutions seeking the expulsion of South Africa from the United Nations. This was a Whitlam initiative, ignoring the doubts of his foreign minister" Don Willesee (Oliver 2010: 482), who believed that this was inconsistent with Australian policy on the recognition of a state's control of territory.

On recognition, there were two main approaches: that control of a territory should be the criterion in determining recognition, versus a view that recognition signals approval and is something that therefore requires consideration of merit (Suter 1975). Since World War II the UK followed the former approach, the US the latter. Interestingly, the UK recognised the Soviets in 1924. Under the foreign policy protocols of the time, that meant that so did Australia. The USA did not recognise the USSR until 1933 under Roosevelt. Prior to Whitlam, Australia adhered to the American approach to recognition and, for example, did not confer recognition to China, North Vietnam, North Korea, East Germany, Rhodesia, or Biafra (Suter 1975: 69). Under Whitlam, "...we have begun to deal with all the countries which satisfy the criteria of statehood. In this we have broken with the policies of our predecessors" (Whitlam 1973b: 337). On 22 December 1972 Australia formally recognised the People's Republic of China and East Germany. In Chile, there was no change in recognition after the coup in September 1973. North Korea was recognised on 31 July 1974. The government activated recognition of various states by setting up embassies in the Bahamas, Barbados, Guatemala, Guinea-Bissau, Guyana, the Holy See, Jamaica, Trinidad and Tobago, Saudi Arabia, Sudan, Venezuela, and Iraq (Suter 1975: 69).

Viviani saw Whitlam's nationalism as distinct, attractive, and non-jingoist: "...[T]his national identity is independent, non-military, anti-racist, region-centred and internationalist" (Viviani 1997: 100). This new regional approach relates to a more nuanced and engaged Asian orientation compared to previous Australian governments. Stephen Fitzgerald, Whitlam's and Australia's first Ambassador to the People's

Republic of China (PRC), said: "...he gave Australia Asia. He wasn't Asia literate in the linguistic sense... [but] in visiting any Asian country for more than a few hours he'd plunge into learning about it and surprise his hosts with his curiosity and knowledge..." (Fitzgerald 2015: 256). Bob Hawke's Foreign Minister, Gareth Evans, in his recalibration, says: "This was a new, much more confident nationalism clearly evident — one easily accepting the need for Australia to form independent judgements..." (Evans 1997: 14). Whitlam preferred to see the point differently. As he said: "Much is written about Australia's 'new nationalism': I would rather put it in terms of Australia's new internationalism" (Quoted, Curran 2004: 130).

When Whitlam was a young man, serving as an airman in the Royal Australian Air Force, U.S. President F.D. Roosevelt and British Prime Minister W.S. Churchill announced on August 14, 1941 'The Atlantic Charter', a statement of aims in seeking to build a new world. This was a formative influence on Whitlam. A statement of common aims, the Charter held that (1) neither nation sought any aggrandizement; (2) they desired no territorial changes without the free assent of the peoples concerned; (3) they respected every people's right to choose its own form of government and wanted sovereign rights and self-government restored to those forcibly deprived of them; (4) they would try to promote equal access for all states to trade and to raw materials; (5) they hoped to promote worldwide collaboration so as to improve labour standards, economic progress, and social security; (6) after the destruction of "Nazi tyranny," they would look for a peace under which all nations could live safely within their boundaries, without fear or want;

(7) under such a peace the seas should be free; and (8) pending a general security through renunciation of force, potential aggressors must be disarmed. The Charter's text was utilised in the declaration of unity opposing the AXIS alliance, signed by 31 nations, including Australia, on 1 January 1942 (Stone 1943; Murphy 2016: 200). Reflecting fidelity to the Atlantic Charter, the rights of small powers were part of Doc. Evatt's foreign policy outlook, such that "...small nations and great, though unequal in power, must be equal in rights" (Ball 1945: viii). Additionally, as Evatt declared: "...the lust for colonial areas is a constant threat to the security of the world and will no longer be tolerated by the public opinion of enlightened peoples." (Evatt 1943: 492). It might be surmised that the liberal internationalist outlook of the Charter stood uneasily with the *real politic* of the post war world, with some of the colonial powers attempting to re-establish their position in Asia, for example. But the reality is that there are always choices to take and tension about national and globalist interests.

On global citizenship, Whitlam saw international legal instruments and equality going together. Hence the advocacy of UN and International Labour Organization treaties, but more than that: "This theme, which requires Australia to act as a good international citizen, has a distinguished history in Indonesia's independence struggle and in post-war relief in Chifley's time, and was certainly crucial to Whitlam's foreign policy in his concern with development, aid, apartheid and human rights issues" (Viviani 1997: 100). As Whitlam declared:

> Australia has been prominent in expressing concern about violations of human rights and upholding the right of all

peoples to live in dignity and freedom... Australia had made known her attitude towards the detention of political prisoners and supported United Nations resolutions condemning the violations of human rights in Chile. We shall mark the 26th anniversary of the Universal Declaration of Human Rights ... by becoming a party to two significant international conventions on the civil rights of women, the 1951 Equal Remuneration Convention and the 1953 Convention on the Political Rights of Women (House of Representatives, *Hansard*, 5 December 1974: 4657.)

On racial discrimination, Whitlam said: "We accept that racism and apartheid, whether in South Africa or elsewhere, must be obliterated" (Whitlam 1975b: 450). Whitlam warned that Australia could not be complacent:

As an island nation of predominantly European inhabitants situated on the edge of Asia, we cannot afford the stigma of racialism... I reaffirmed our intention to ratify the 1965 International Convention on the Elimination of All Forms of Racial Discrimination... Our decision to deny racially selected sports teams the right to visit or transit [through] Australia should also be seen in this light... (Whitlam 1973c: 342).

Whitlam in Opposition had interesting things to say about Australian focus and priorities. Without exhaustively surveying this field, some references suffice. In August 1954, he became the first Australian MP to urge recognition of China (Whitlam 1985: 53). In 1960, he argued that: "Australia's foreign policy was arid and unbalanced... our weakest links [in Asia] are with India and Indonesia, the two most populous and advanced countries in that area" (SMH 1960: 5). He also called for a public debate on foreign policy. He wanted a better educated and informed

Australian electorate. In 1964, along with another backbencher and future prime minister, Whitlam and Malcolm Fraser spent two months on a visit to the United States as part of a bi-partisan delegation. At one point, Whitlam commended Sir Garfield Barwick (1903-1997; Minister for External Affairs, 1961-1964), "as one of the very few Ministers who had tried to understand Indonesia's fear of being surrounded and dismembered. Barwick had tried to get Indonesia and Malaysia to talk together" (SMH 1964). This was a theme he returned to, accusing the Coalition government of neglect: "Our relations with Indonesia, the degree to which we can live co-operatively with Indonesia, represent incomparably the most important task for Australian statesmanship for the next century" (SMH 1970: 12). He honed his thinking over many years. Hence:

> Long before 1972 his policy signals were there: the US alliance as one major element of policy, but not the dominant core; the recognition of China; the opposition to the military commitment to Vietnam; the importance attached to Indonesia (seen in his opposition to the government's and Arthur Calwell's stance [which favoured self-determination rather than annexation as part of Indonesia] on West New Guinea [Irian Jaya]); his focus on international instruments and human rights; independence for Papua New Guinea; and the end of the White Australia policy (Viviani 1997: 101).

In Opposition, Whitlam regularly visited the region. As he put the challenge: "[W]hat *does* constitute a foreign policy is striking and keeping a balance between a nation's power and its commitment. This essentially means that a nation must recognise itself for what it is, should be, and can be." Then he went on, saying:

> Australia and Australia's foreign policy makers have scarcely even attempted to answer these questions, because, perhaps, they are regarded as questions for the poet rather than the diplomat or the politician. Yet if we cannot answer these basic questions about ourselves, how shall we answer the more grandiloquent questions about 'national interest', or 'national security' – not to mention 'national destiny'? I do not pretend that the Australian Labor Party has all the answers. I intend at least that we shall make an Australia in which they will be asked (Whitlam 1973a: viii).

Answering those questions was the essence of Whitlamism in foreign policy.

Before becoming prime minister, Whitlam wrote: "Australia is indeed a lucky country. The foreign policy of this nation is in ruins; the foundations on which it rested for more than twenty years have crumbled. Yet we pass on with scarcely a tremor of alarm or a gesture of remorse" (Whitlam 1972: 1). The conservative realist and strategic policy scholar Coral Bell thought so too, describing 1969-72 as a period when the Australian government could be characterised as having an "incapacity to adapt, intellectual blankness, and psychological paralysis" as the foreign policy settings were changing around them (Bell 1977: 189). In anticipation of electoral victory, Whitlam said: "We have been given a second chance. Few countries have been granted as much." (Whitlam 1972: 19). In fashioning a new course, he was opposed to being "timid" (Whitlam 1975b: 450).

Whitlam regarded the South-East Asia Treaty Organisation (SEATO) alliance formed in 1954 as redundant. W.L. Morrison described SEATO as a "camouflaged corpse".

(Hudson 1972: 115). Last rites followed in 1977 after most members lost interest and withdrew. The Australian presence in Singapore and Malaysia also came under review. Whitlam said: "We believe that our pledge to uphold the Five Power [Defence] Arrangements [FPDA – i.e., with Australia, the UK, Malaysia, Singapore, and New Zealand] does not require the stationing of forces abroad on permanent garrison duty for its redemption" (Whitlam 1973c: 339). Australia had originally stationed troops in Malaysia in 1955 and then, from 1957, around two to three thousand Australians were stationed there (van der Kroef 1970: 11). On 1 January 1975, the three-nation ANZUK force, based in Singapore, ceased to exist. (AFAR 1975: 44). Singapore blamed Australia for the break-up of the ANZUK forces. (Johns 1974). Singapore, a mere "little red dot island-nation" (Kho & Li Lin, 2005), relied on allies to be stable and close, as if felt vulnerable, with zero strategic depth, to potential defence threats. (Singapore still trains its defence forces in Taiwan – arrangements made in the 1960s and "accepted" by China in normalising relations with Singapore in 1990 – as well as in Australia, and relies on informal protections from Medium and Great Power interests. Singapore's airforce is largely trained in Australia.) Interestingly, under Whitlam, the Royal Malaysian Air Force (RMAF) Base, Butterworth, situated on the northwest coast of the Malaysian State of Penang, eight kilometres east of its capital, George Town, continued. The base is the headquarters of the Five Power Defence Arrangements Integrated Area Defence System (HQIADS). Since World War II, Australia had prided itself about being a reliable ally, though arguably not as independently minded under the Coalition with respect to the

US. But here was an instance of Australia's reliability to several key Asian allies being in question. (Whitlam never explicitly argued this point, but he considered that the presence of Australian troops was a potential affront to Indonesia, given *Konfrontasi*, "confrontation" and fighting between Malaysia and Indonesia over northern Borneo in 1963-66.) In Asia as much as with the US, Australia is at pains to demonstrate reliability, just as Australia sometimes worries about the reliability of others towards itself. This is a key piece of the Whitlam legacy, including for the ALP, with Singapore and Malaysia. The Singaporeans and the Malaysians were highly critical of Whitlam's stance on the FPDA and withdrawing Australian troops – and how it was done.

On Australia's representation as a guest at meetings of the Non-Aligned Movement, Whitlam explained:

> We are not moving into anybody's orbit... There is nothing incompatible between our policy... No one has suggested that Australia was seeking to become a Latin American country because it welcomed the opportunity to attend the last meeting of the Organisation of American States in Washington as an observer (Whitlam 1973c: 338).

Willesee explained that "attendance at major non-aligned meetings would provide for gaining a closer and deeper understanding of the policies and aspirations of non-aligned countries, both individually and collectively" (Willesee 1975: 446). He preferred that Australia be a guest rather than an observer, lest there be any confusion as to Australia's position concerning its alliance relationships.

In a February 1975 summation of his government's policy

achievement, Whitlam declared:

> ...Australia ha[s] at last got her relations right with the 4 powers of most immediate concern to us – with Indonesia, our nearest neighbour; with Japan, our largest trading partner; with China, the most populous nation on earth; and with the United States, the world's most powerful nation and our firmest ally. My visit to China ended a generation of lost contact with a quarter of the world's people (Whitlam 1975a: 69).

The policy context is important: *détente* between the two major superpowers, the US-Sino rapprochement, the running sore of Vietnam coming to an end, the implications of Nixon's Guam doctrine. The latter refers to President Nixon's call, in a speech delivered in Guam on 24 July 1969, that allies need to provide for their own self-defence and to only expect American support in extreme circumstances. This ultimately led to the US policy of "Vietnamisation" and to a greater understanding by US allies of the need for greater self-reliance in defence. But at the time, it engendered significant policy uncertainty (Murphy 1973: 331; White 2019).

After Whitlam's first year in office, foreign policy correspondent Peter Hastings (1920-1990), opined:

> In the end, after a year of Whitlamism, we have been offered some brilliant and salutary initiatives in foreign affairs, but we have nothing as yet approaching a foreign policy. Mr Whitlam has whistled some exciting, disparate and long-awaited tunes. He needs now to orchestrate them into respectable music (Hastings 1973: 6).

This complaint echoed other assessments. Such as in the statement that "... a small power, whose foreign and defence policies depend so much on the unpredictable intentions and actions of other states, must find it difficult to develop long term coherent policies" (Palfreeman 1972: 121). Developing a coherent policy depended upon an understanding of the nation's interests and values, and objectives to pursue.

Whitlam was in the process of developing his approach to many challenges, repositioning in the context of a changing world, responding to "events", and in Acheson's words finessing the capacity for good decision-making. Hastings thought Whitlam's positions on China, moves towards the NARA Agreement with Japan (formally known as the Basic Treaty of Friendship and Co-operation between Australia and Japan, eventually signed by Malcolm Fraser in June 1976) and relatively small but important moves like Whitlam's attendance at the Pacific Forum meeting in Apia, Fiji, were immensely important in establishing a credible style and substantive approach to policy. (Australia had previously only been represented at the Pacific Forum by a junior minister, Charles Edward "Ceb" Barnes (1901-98), the Country Party MP and Minister for External Territories, at the inaugural 1971 Forum meeting.) Whitlam thought he should show support by attending as Prime Minister (Hastings 1973: 6). Whitlam argued: "We should be the natural leaders of the South Pacific" (Clark 1974: 7). His example was followed by regular prime ministerial attendance of his successors at South Pacific Forum meetings.

Whitlam attending a United Nations meeting during a visit to the United States of America in 1974. Photograph: National Archives of Australia.

Perceptively, Viviani thought: "Whitlam was able to change, decisively, the foreign policy climate in Australia." In doing so, "Whitlam broke the conceptual grid of previous governments' Cold War policies in the minds of most Australians, and this was perhaps his greatest achievement" (Viviani 1997: 102). The insight espoused by Whitlam and emphasised by all Labor governments thereafter was that the region itself is not threatening. Whitlamism oversaw the end of "forward defence" and beginning of common security in the region. As Hawke expressed the point: "Australia should seek security 'in and with Asia, not against it'" (Woolcott 2018: 14). This point was particularly emphasised during Paul Keating's prime ministry when he repeatedly said Australia seeks security *in* Asia, not *from* Asia (Keating 1995: 187-224; especially, Keating 1996).

Andrew Peacock, the Opposition spokesperson on foreign affairs during Whitlam's prime ministership, argued that Whitlam's policy positioning was messy. More pointedly, "there is inconsistency and incoherence in the very substance of his policy: between the American alliance and the 'even-handed' approach to the Indian Ocean" (Peacock 1974). The Opposition supported the expansion and upgrade of the joint US/UK military base established on the island of Diego Garcia, in the Indian Ocean. They claimed Whitlam's support of a nuclear-free "zone of peace" in the Indian Ocean clashed with American interests and undermined the Australian-America alliance (Albinski 1977: 254-56). There is evidence that the Americans were concerned about Australian attitudes. ASEAN and India, as well as governments in countries supportive of the non-aligned movement, were in favour of the Indian Ocean as a "zone of peace". Interestingly, in July 1973, a discussion between the Shah of Iran, Dr Henry Kissinger, the then US National Security Adviser, and Richard Helms, the then US Ambassador to Iran, turned to the Indian Ocean and the purchase of an American destroyer by Iran. The Americans wanted the Soviets to know that US allies would match any efforts of the USSR to commit naval resources to the region. The transcript reveals the Shah said to Kissinger: "…even Mr Whitlam will have to change his view." To which Kissinger replied: "Especially Whitlam. What we want to do is to get our allies into a frame of mind where they feel that they have more to lose than we do when they criticize us and take us to task" (MoC 1973: pp. 8-9). Whitlam mentions in his memoirs that he expressed misgivings to President Ford about the further development of military facilities there when they met in Washington in 1974 (Whitlam 1985: 48). Owen Harries, informal consultant to Peacock prior to the latter's appointment as Foreign Minister after the demise of the Whitlam government at the end of 1975, also contended that the Whitlam position on Diego Garcia represented infidelity towards the Americans (Harries 1975b: 1091). Both Peacock and Harries could have developed their arguments into something more persuasive; they came close to implying *any* disagreement with American policy could only be in bad faith, a subservient position that they did not articulate otherwise. As Harries was to say in 2002: "…perhaps Australia is too keen on tokenism with the United States, and too eager to be part of everything. Australia …should act with discrimination" (Harries & Windybank 2002: 280).

The next section covers Whitlam's initiatives and responses in five areas of policy initiative: China, Papua New Guinea (PNG), the ANZUS alliance, the American defence bases, and Indonesia. These were five conspicuous hallmarks of Whitlam's game-changing diplomatic initiative, notwithstanding East Timor, which is considered. This discussion is followed by an issue arguably of no great importance, Whitlam's "trips". Next, Whitlam's controversies, where dubious and foolish positions were taken on Vietnam, Timor, recognition of the Baltic States, and stances on the Middle East, are examined. There were areas where disappointments, mistakes, and misjudgements served to sully Whitlam's reputation. Finally, and additionally, the Iraqi party loans affair deserves mentioning because of its implications for policy had Whitlam been re-elected in 1975.

Senator Don Willesee, Australian Foreign Minister, 6 November 1973 – 11 November 1975. Photo circa 1974.

Five Hallmarks

Dr Rex Patterson, MP, then Opposition Spokesperson on Primary Industry and Northern Development; Opposition Leader Gough Whitlam; and Chinese Premier Zhou Enlai, with interpreter behind him, in Beijing in June 1971.

China

Nine days before Kissinger's visit, nine months before Nixon's, Australian Opposition Leader Whitlam visited China in July 1971. "On no diplomatic issue has the McMahon government suffered more embarrassment than that of relations with China" (Hudson 1972: 113). On 12 July 1971 Liberal Prime Minister McMahon boasted: "In no time at all Zhou Enlai had Mr Whitlam on a hook and he played him as a fisherman plays a trout" (Mullins 2018: 435). McMahon "was left uninformed" of Nixon's strategy, announced with Kissinger's trip to Beijing 9-11 July 1971, to open diplomatic channels to China (Woodard 2018: 172). Within weeks, the Americans announced a China strategy that made Australian conservatives look awkward and locked into an out-of-date policy paradigm. Margaret Whitlam remembered: "Gough could not stop himself from laughing at [McMahon's] gaffe. Neither could the media" (Mitchell 2006: 183). Recognition of the Peoples' Republic of China was conferred by Prime Minister Whitlam on 22 December 1972. Australia "acknowledged" China's claim to Taiwan. In contrast, in October 1970 the Canadians "took note" of the claim (Clark 1974: 8). Would it have been wiser to "note" rather than "acknowledge" China's claim to Taiwan? Stephen Fitzgerald, who had learnt Chinese in Taiwan in 1964 understood that in the previous three hundred years "the island was only nominally ruled by the Chinese government" (Fitzgerald 2015: 34). The Chinese pressed for stronger wording than what they got from the Canadians a few years before. Both the People's Republic of China and the Republic of China on Taiwan had campaigned for full recognition of their claim to be the legitimate government of all of China. The word "acknowledge" is stronger than "note" as the former can mean "accept the validity or legitimacy of" (*Oxford English Dictionary*). The Americans too, on 27 February 1972, in the *Joint Communiqué of the United States of America and the People's Republic of China*, also known as the *Shanghai Communiqué*, formally *acknowledged* that "all Chinese on either side of the Taiwan Strait maintain there is but one China" (Chen, 1979; see Kissinger 1994: 726-730). This document was signed by Nixon during his visit to Beijing in February 1972. Beforehand,

Mao promised no military conquest, saying: "The small issue is Taiwan; the big issue is the world" (Kissinger: 726).

Taiwan was yet to develop into a thriving democracy. In 1972 Chiang Kai-shek (1887-1975) ruled the island under martial law. But that was not the end of Australian considerations. Perceptively, on future Australian-Taiwanese relations, in a 1 April 1973 memo to Australian Ambassador Fitzgerald, Whitlam wrote:

> Present Chinese thinking appears to be against armed action and in favour of liberation by 'people's diplomacy'. We hope that this policy will continue and be successful. In the meantime, we intend to be quite firm in insisting that private trade and travel between Australia and Taiwan should continue. To use Peking's own argument, we have nothing against the people of Taiwan (Curran 2022: 36).

Fitzgerald himself confidently proclaimed: "[Australia] is able to contemplate a rational relationship with China, independent, and free from the neuroses of the Cold War" (Fitzgerald 1973: 176). More realistically: "Whitlam's China initiative involved a felicitous combination of timing, courage and luck" (Freudenberg 1993: 202). Fitzgerald recognised it was luck that made the visit appear prescient or well-judged – Whitlam visiting in 1971, just before Kissinger: "But the ALP move was grounded on a policy which had been debated and endorsed by the party..." (Fitzgerald 1972: 15). China was still a strange place. Deng Xiaoping (1904-1997) remained banished to the countryside as a worker at the Xinjian County Tractor Factory in rural Jiangxi province. The disastrous Chinese Cultural Revolution was unsubdued. Reform prospects looked unpromising. In 1972, Deng's apology to Mao led to the possibility of a return from exile to Beijing. In 1973, Premier Zhou Enlai (1898-1976) brought Deng back to Zhongnanhai, the central government compound, to focus on reconstructing the Chinese economy. Whitlam, based on his meeting with Mao in early November 1973, recollected that: "[Mao] lacked Zhou's grasp of detail and incomparable knowledge of particular events and personalities, but his wisdom and sense of history were deep and unmistakeable" (Whitlam 1985: 59). It was wise for Australia along with other nations in the 1970s, the United States particularly, to belatedly cultivate healthy diplomatic relations with the Peoples' Republic of China. But given Mao's murderous legacy, his "wisdom" is an odd thing to note in celebratory terms.

On Whitlam's second trip to Beijing, as prime minister, he proposed to Zhou Enlai: "There should be consultations between Australia and China as close and significant as we have traditionally had with Britain and the United States and similar to discussions we now have annually with Japan at ministerial level and with the Soviet Union at the officials' level." In writing that, Australian Ambassador Fitzgerald noted that the then head of the Australian Department of Foreign Affairs, Sir Keith Waller (1914-1992), looked at the ceiling as Whitlam said those words. Whitlam's statement expressed the beginnings of Australia's desire to know China well, to act as a bridge in explaining China to allies, and to forge a creative relationship, without being either uncritical, doting, or hostile. That remains Australia's ambition today.

Australian Ambassador Stephen FitzGerald (right) and then Australian prime minister Gough Whitlam meet Chairman Mao Tse-tung on 2 November 1973, in Beijing.

Of one thing there can be no doubt. Whitlam's realism about recognition was consistent throughout his political life. As he said in the debate on international affairs in the parliament on 12 August 1954:

> We must recognise the fact that the government installed in Formosa [the name for Taiwan coined by the Portuguese] has no chance of ever again becoming the government of China unless it is enabled to do so as a result of a third world war. When we say that that government should be the government of China, we not only take an unrealistic view but a menacing one. The Australian Government should have recognised the Communist Government in China, in view of the fact that all our neighbours, including the colonial powers, Great Britain and the Netherlands, have recognised it. (House of Representatives, *Hansard*, 21st Parliament, 1st Session, 12 August 1954).

Labor policy, from 1955, had been to recognise the PRC. On this score alone – initiative, boldness, and long-term impact – the visit to China in 1971 and return as prime minister in 1973 marked Whitlam's importance as one of the greatest of Australia's foreign ministers.

As a side note, on a subsequent visit to China, Gough and Margaret Whitlam were in Tientsin, an hour's drive from Beijing, on 28 July 1976 when a severe earthquake hit at night (Mitchell 2006: 291-293). Peter Nicholson composed a cartoon, decried by some as in poor taste:

Nicholson's cartoon on the morning after the earthquake the night before, late July 1976. (Reproduced with the permission of the Nicholson family).

Whitlam purchased the original, framed it, and hung it over the marital bed. As Peter Hartcher, the *Sydney Morning Herald* journalist wrote in 2014: "The Whitlams had a sense of humour. And Gough was entirely at home with great tectonic shifts" (Hartcher 2014).

Papua New Guinea (PNG)

Whitlam once declared: "If history were to obliterate the whole of my public career, save my contribution to the independence of a democratic PNG, I should rest content" (Whitlam 1985: 101; highlighted in Wong 2022). He had visited six times before becoming prime minister.

It was not until June 1971 that the ALP's National Conference declared that "the Labor Party will ensure the orderly and secure transfer to PNG of self-government and independence in its first term of office" (Denoon 2012: 104). In an essay on the policies of a future Labor administration, Whitlam wrote that Australia had to anticipate and get ahead of any separatist or PNG independence movement: "The most effective way of stopping the growth of separatism is to create an independent Papua New Guinea as quickly as possible" (Whitlam 1972: 16). Interestingly, however, nothing of that kind was directly said in Whitlam's policy speech or McMahon's in late 1972 to commit either party to acceleration of independence. But within two and a half years, independence was granted on 16 September 1975, even if the new country, economically, remained "a client state" of Australia's (Standish 1976: 107). The contrary argument to this "success" of independence is the assessment that independence was thrust upon PNG to avoid the UN characterising Australia as a colonial power. On this view, PNG was not properly prepared for independence. Another related perspective is that the campaign for independence was "used by an educated elite obsessed with and overwhelmed by the rush to take over political and economic power" (Sirox Kari 2005: 3). Given subsequent failures of governance, the proposition was proffered that Australia could have better helped PNG ready itself beforehand. But to this author, arguments for delay are unpersuasive and would have tested Australian-PNG relations – potentially, to a disastrous breaking point. Independence was achieved without much rancour and with the support of the local, self-governing PNG Assembly (Griffin et. al. 1979: 178-235). A fair assessment is: "Papua New Guinea since Independence is neither a triumph nor a tragedy. It has done some things better than most foreigners expected – the critics of Independence in 1975, but also the promoters of Independence in Australia's national interest" (Garnaut 2000: 35).

Bill Morrison (1928-2013), Minister in the Whitlam government, including as Minister for External Territories, later Ambassador to Indonesia 1985-1989, commented in 1987 that his personal highlight in politics was achieving independence for Papua New Guinea. He quoted the PNG Governor-General Sir John Guise who said: "The Australian flag was not torn down but came down with honour" (SMH 1987: 12). Morrison's heading of a chapter in a book on Whitlam stated a reasonable conclusion: "Papua New Guinea: A Quiet Achievement" (Morrison 2013). One part of this achievement was that despite some reservations about "haste", the Opposition was mostly supportive of Whitlam's PNG policy.

PNG's new Prime Minister, Michael Somare, chats with his Australian counterpart Gough Whitlam while waiting for the formal ceremony to begin, on the day of PNG's independence, when the Australian flag was lowered in Port Moresby, 16 September 1975. Photograph: National Archives of Australia.

ANZUS

The American alliance was severely tested in the first six months of Whitlam's prime ministership. Yet, as Whitlam pronounced:

> The maintenance of our alliance with the United States under ANZUS remains most important for our security, since by its very nature it has created and guarantees in the Pacific a zone of peace in which the peoples of the region have for the last 20 years been free to pursue their political, economic and social goals without fear of hostile intervention or attack. The ANZUS Treaty reflects a natural relationship between these countries of the Pacific. Its continuation is not questioned by any of its partners (Whitlam 1973c: 341).

That, however, was said after a fraught period of Australia being in the 'deep freeze'.

Before coming to that, it is interesting that Whitlam strove in his Opposition period to forge close relations with the United States. Four photos tell a story.

The first shows Whitlam and President L.B. Johnson on 14 June 1967 on the White House lawn, with Miss Irrigation and Miss Hydro Power. This was less than two months after Whitlam was elected Leader of the Opposition. He was understandably anxious, given the strength of feeling of support in Australia for the American alliance, to show he could develop a working relationship with an American President. Harold Holt (1908-1967), in June 1966, on a visit to the White House, declared "all the way with LBJ" – a reprise of Johnson's winning presidential election slogan in 1964.

Johnson had become friends with Holt and visited Australia 20-23 October 1966, the first incumbent American President to do so. One can imagine that Whitlam's 1967 visit and his meeting with Johnson, as having been grudgingly conceded. Does the photo tell all there needs to be said? In fact, no; although any meeting, slotted into the President's itinerary, albeit with a bevy of beauties unrelated to Australia, was better than no meeting at all, this was only one of a series of meetings over a four hour stretch that day between the Australian Opposition Leader and the US President. The Americans saw Whitlam as a moderating influence within the ALP. As Whitlam's speechwriter Graham Freudenberg said of his speeches written for both Calwell and Whitlam: "All these speeches wrestled with an insoluble dilemma: how to oppose American intervention in Vietnam without opposing America; how to denounce the war without denouncing the United States" (Freudenberg 2006: 59; Whitlam expresses a comparable perspective: Whitlam 1981: 62-63). As Christine Wallace remarks, thinking of Freudenberg's discussion of Whitlam's approach to the Vietnam War: "Vietnam was not just the name of a country or a war but the name of an epoch" (Wallace 2024: 149).

Thanks to Troy Bramston's sleuthing, he revealed 49 years later some of the details of Whitlam and Johnson time together that day: two hours in the Oval Office, a meeting approved by Australian Prime Minister Harold Holt, who was to see Johnson himself at the President's ranch a few days later in Texas. After their lengthy discussion, Whitlam and Johnson then went to the White House lawn where hundreds had gathered under the auspices of the Rural Electrification Administration (REA).

The caption read: President Johnson and E.G. Whitlam, leader of the Australian Labor Party, have two pretty girls beside them today [14 June 1967] at a meeting on the White House lawn of young people representing rural electrification systems. The girls are from left: Patricia van Haaften of Tucson, Ariz, Miss REA [Rural Electrification Administration], and Kathy Crusty of Aurora, Colo., National Grange Princess. Source: American Press Wire Photo.

An LBJ badge, widely circulated during the 1964 US Presidential election campaign. Source: public domain.

(Whitlam 1985: 38). The REA program, created in May 1935 by President Roosevelt as part of the "New Deal", allowed the federal government to make low-cost loans to farmers who had banded together to create non-profit cooperatives for the purpose of bringing electricity to rural America. Johnson utilised the REA in winning support and building his base (Caro 1994: 251-252; 277; 285). Interestingly, Whitlam's memoir mentions his meeting, but not how long and comprehensive were those nearly four hours. Before the REA attendees, from the stage, Johnson said: "We have a very distinguished visitor with us this morning who, I know, will enjoy you, and I think you would want to know. He is the young and brilliant leader of the Australian Labor Party" (Bramston 2015). Immediately afterwards, Johnson and Whitlam met the evangelist, the Rev. Billy Graham. Whitlam and Johnson seemed to have hit it off. The second photo shows Johnson and Whitlam in earnest discussion at the White House. Though a topic for another place. The tragedy of Johnson's administration was that one of the greatest, reforming US Presidents, grandly focused on civil rights and the Great Society, would be imperilled, and destroyed politically by the Vietnam War. Robert Caro's fifth and final – forthcoming – volume of his biography of Johnson, will undoubtedly explain why and how. Vietnam affected everyone and everything in the political process in that time.

Whitlam in the Oval Office with President Johnson, 14 June 1967. Photograph from the National Archives of Australia.

The third photo is from Whitlam's visit to the White House on 30 July 1973, after President Nixon reversed plans not to meet the Australian Prime Minister. There was tension and some warmth established, but Nixon remained suspicious, coming so soon after Whitlam's criticisms of the US's conduct of the Vietnam War, earlier in his prime ministry, as analysed below.

Prime Minister Whitlam and President Nixon discuss world events and Australian-US relations, The Oval Office, The White House, 30 July 1973. Source: American Press Wirephoto.

The fourth photograph shows Whitlam, President Ford, and Henry Kissinger, in an apparently relaxed pose. By now, Whitlam was regarded with more respect compared to his visit to the White House under President Nixon. The *New York Times* reported that aides called the meeting a "low-keyed and amiable chat". The White House press secretary, Ron Nessen, said there was "an exchange of views on global and regional problems" (NYT 1974: 29).

Whitlam, President Ford, and US Secretary of State Henry Kissinger, 4 October 1974. Source: American Press Wirephoto.

All three meetings with those US Presidents occurred in the context of the Vietnam War.

Nixon's wariness, even animosity, was due to actions of the Whitlam government soon after coming to power.

In December 1972, Whitlam announced that all remaining Australian advisers would be withdrawn from South Vietnam. By then, 148 were all that remained (Bell 1988: 117). Labor on 27 December 1972 announced cancellation of military aid to South Vietnam and abandoned training of their and Cambodian troops in Australia. Condemnation by Australian government ministers, mainly from the Left, attacking American bombing raids on Hanoi, Haiphong, and other North Vietnamese targets in Indo-China at Christmas time 1972 and in early 1973 infuriated Nixon. Whitlam wrote a letter to the American President expressing opposition to what he deemed was excessive American firepower and wrong-headed strategy. (For the text of his letter, Whitlam 1985: 42-43). After the 27 January 1973 Paris Vietnamese Peace Agreement was unveiled, on 26 February Australia announced recognition of North Vietnam, without consulting with the Americans (Hearder 2016: 147). In March 1973 President Nixon ordered that no Cabinet member was to meet with Australian officials. He made it known that he would not meet Whitlam when he planned to visit Washington mid-year. As is now better appreciated via historian James Curran's book *Unholy Fury. Whitlam and Nixon at War* (2015), the hostility in Washington towards Whitlam was at boiling point.

Whitlam telephoned Ross Terrill, an Australian academic at Harvard, who knew Henry Kissinger, to obtain an audience for Peter Wilenski (1939-94), Whitlam's chief of staff, with Kissinger, which occurred in early May 1973. This was aimed at smoothing the waters for a meeting with the US President. Near contemporaneously, Opposition Shadow Foreign Minister Andrew Peacock on a visit in June to Washington, met George H.W. Bush, then Chair of the Republican National Committee, and US Vice President Spiro Agnew. Peacock made it clear that refusing to meet Whitlam might be harmful to both Australian and American interests and could dangerously undermine support for the alliance in Australia. They conveyed the message to the White House.

Sir James Plimsoll (1917-1987), whose many diplomatic assignments included Head of the Department of Foreign Affairs, 1965-70, Ambassador to the United States, 1970-1973, and Ambassador to the Soviet Union, 1973-1977, tried to assuage impressions by members of the Nixon administration and the President himself that the Whitlam government could not be trusted. With Whitlam, "the danger was actually more apparent than real" (Bell 1988b: 144).

Whitlam met Nixon on 30 July 1973, in a 40-minute meeting. Nixon was persuaded it was best to get to know his counterpart. But each was wary of the other. Whitlam quipped that Nixon had J.D. Ehrlichman, the White House Counsel and adviser to the President, and H.R. Halderman, the White House Chief of Staff, known as "The Berlin Wall", whereas he had a "Polish Corridor" – a reference to Wilenski and Jim Spigelman, Whitlam's principal private secretary; both were Jewish, both born in Poland (Email exchange, *Michael Easson and Jim Spigelman*, 27 January 2023). The next day, Nixon mused to Japanese prime minister Tanaka his fears about a mood towards isolationism in the US and among allies. Curran suggests that there was a "...gulf between Nixon's guiding philosophy of realism and what he saw as the woolly-headed thinking of idealistic liberal internationalists" (Curran 2015: 248). Yet while both leaders distinguished themselves by recognising the emerging, more complex post-Vietnam world, it seems they never got to know each other. But, Clark suggests the Americans and Australians developed better mutual understanding about Australian nationalism which was not "anti-American but pro-Australian" (Clark 1974: 4).

There is merit in the assessment that: "Plimsoll had, through his judicious counsel, unflagging and well-targeted advocacy in Washington, and adroit mediation between American and Australian prima donna leaders, protected the valuables in the relationship during an unprecedented period of turbulence" (Hearder: 160). Most important for the Americans, on a realist perspective particularly, was consideration of their defence assets in Australia and how best to retain and protect them.

Bases

The question as to whether all US defence facilities on Australian soil should be jointly managed by both countries was one of the most vexed issues for the Whitlam government. It was also one of the most successful examples of Whitlam managing his party, explaining, and justifying a position to the public, and achieving practical outcomes that respected Australian sovereignty that won admiration even in Washington.

In March 1963, at the famous "faceless men" meeting (Fitzgerald & Holt 2010: 152-164), Australian Labor Leader Arthur Calwell (1896-1973), Leader, 1960-1967, sought a favourable ruling from the ALP Federal Conference on the North-West Cape facility which was carried 19-17 (Whitlam 1985: 33). The base, since renamed the Harold E. Holt Naval Communication Station in Western Australia, is on the Indian Ocean, 6 km north of the town of Exmouth.

Not that the 1963 ALP Conference resolution constituted whole-hearted support of the party. Beazley notes that the debate then and later was important in reorienting Australian Labor away from neutralist viewpoints of the Left: "... this debate shifted Labor's foreign policy from a non-aligned tendency to a commitment to the US alliance" (K.C. Beazley 2016: 210). Because of the ALP splits between 1955-1957, for

"…a time the party's Left, who were sceptical of the alliance, dominated organisational policy outcomes despite the fact that a majority of the Parliamentary Caucus disagreed with their line" (K.C. Beazley 2016: 210). Freudenberg highlights some of the tensions: "Foreign affairs became the line of division not only between two parties, but between the Labor factions" (Freudenberg 1993: 204).

Interestingly, one of Whitlam's former staffers, John Menadue (principal private secretary to Whitlam, 1960-67, and later head of the Department of Prime Minister and Cabinet, 1975-76), criticised the obsessive secrecy that the Menzies government encouraged: "On the instruction of Prime Minister Menzies and with the connivance of [Labor Opposition Leader] Arthur Calwell, [Whitlam] was refused briefings on ASIS [Australian Secret Intelligence Service] and the Defence Signals Department" (Menadue 1999: 133). Without detracting from the gist of Menadue's point, the then DSD (now Australian Signals Directorate) was previously the Defence Signals Branch and the Defence Signals Division, but never a 'Department'.

In 1972, there was ambiguity on what Labor might do. The 1972 ALP Policy Platform was a compromise between the hostile and accommodating. The policy 'On Joint Facilities and US Bases and Facilities', read:

> Labor is opposed to the existence of foreign-owned, -controlled or -operated bases and facilities in Australian territory, especially if such bases involve a derogation from Australian sovereignty.
>
> Labor is not opposed to the use of Australian bases and facilities by Allies in war-time, or in periods of international

tension involving a threat to Australia, provided that Australian authority and sovereignty are unimpaired, and provided that Australia is not involved in hostilities without Australia's consent.

The tenure of these bases and facilities by other powers should not be of such a character as to exclude properly accredited access by authorised Australians charged with the duty of evaluating Australian defence policy, whether members of the Australian Parliament, defence departments or armed services.

(*Complete Guide to Labor's Policies* 1972: 44-45).

In Whitlam's November 1972 Policy Speech, he promised to renegotiate terms with the Americans. Freudenberg pointed out: "In March 1973, [Whitlam] headed off moves originating in the Victorian branch to revise party policy on the presence of American bases by asserting that such a change would be a breach of the mandate" (Freudenberg 1993: 205). The saying at the time, attributed to Kim E. Beazley (1917-2007), Whitlam minister, 1972-1975, was that the Platform was the Old Testament, the Policy Speech the New Testament. This was a neat way to thwart any moves by the Left to hijack or disrupt Whitlam's authority to deal with this issue.

Labor did what it pledged to do – renegotiate the treaties which set up various bases, turning them into joint facilities. Global strategist Coral Bell noted that the bases at North-West Cape, Pine Gap, and Nurrungar were "part of the complex system of *command, control, communications, and intelligence* necessary for the United States to match and outmatch the Soviet Union..." (emphasis in the original) (Bell 1988b: 142).

Whitlam greeted by President Nixon at the White House, 30 July 1973, with Dr Kissinger (obscured) to the left. Photograph: Nixon Presidential Library.

Did the negotiations lead to substantive or trivial change? One contemporary assessment was "...it was on this issue that it became clear how little real change the government was prepared to contemplate in the fundamental defence alliance, however audacious ministers might be at a verbal level" (Goldsworthy 1974a: 106). This view, however, downplays what was achieved, which was significant.

After all, "… it had been virtually ingrained in the DNA of Washington's foreign policy establishment that Labor posed serious difficulties for the alliance – that, in effect, it was spoiling to expel the US intelligence facilities from Australian soil" (Curran 2015: 311). As Bell acidly comments: "…it is impossible entirely to dismiss the idea that behind the scenes in Washington, some backroom boy deep in the bureaucracy of the intelligence communities was interpreting or misinterpreting these early signals from Canberra to somewhat alarmist effect." (Bell 1988a: 121).

In his memoirs, Sir Arthur Tange (1914-2001), secretary of the Department of External Affairs, 1954-65, and of the Department of Defence, 1970-1979, discusses the controversy on the Joint US-Australian defence facilities, including the Joint Defence Space Research Facility at Pine Gap near Alice Springs, and the Joint Defence Space Communications Facility at Nurrungar near Woomera in the north of South Australia, which included early warning surveillance (Tange 2008: 69-79). Lance Barnard (1919-1997), the Deputy Prime Minister and Minister for Defence, 1972-1975, under Whitlam, argued that the bases were useful in monitoring conformity with Test Ban treaties. Tange noted that what Ministers and officials could say publicly was limited: "They remained shackled by the limited amount of information they could disclose in order to satisfy party and public" (Tange: 73).

Whitlam explained why the government supported the facilities:

> Prompt, reliable, and comprehensive information is vital to the maintenance of global peace and security. We have previously

informed the public that the Joint Defence Space Research Facility at Pine Gap near Alice Springs and the Joint Defence Space Communications station at Nurrungar are related to satellites and that they analyse and test data. We. have also stated that neither installation is part of a weapons system, and neither can be used to attack any country, and we have been convinced that they contribute specifically to the improvement and development of Australia's defence system (Whitlam 1973c: 342).

But he also said: "The Government still has certain reservations about the United States Naval Communication Station at North-West Cape and it is our intention to seek a renegotiation of the original terms of the agreement establishing this station in Australia" (Whitlam 1973c: 342). When the Yom Kippur War broke out in October 1973, Whitlam was unsure how the American facilities in Australia were being used. In January 1974, Barnard went to Washington, where the Americans agreed Amberley and the Alice Springs facilities would be totally under Australian control, and an Australian would be second in command at the North-West Cape (Goldsworthy 1974a). The agreement went further than that. The Australian defence and security academic Des Ball (1947-2016) explained: "Following discussions in Washington between Defence Minister Barnard and [US] Defense Secretary Schlesinger, it was agreed that the Royal Australian Navy would increase its use of the station for its communications with surface and submarine vessels; that some 35 Australian service personnel would be stationed at the facility to assist" (D. Ball 1980: 56).

Additionally: "Willesee presided over the 1975 renegotiation of the agreement between Australia and the United States regarding the American communications base at North-West Cape, under which the facility would now be operated jointly" (Oliver 2010: 482). Interestingly, the facilities are now more than defensive in their operations, as they are intimately integrated into American strategic defence operations – the implications of which are greater than what can now be covered here.

Indonesia

Throughout his long career, Whitlam highlighted the overriding importance of achieving closer relations with Indonesia. This was a bi-partisan objective. Foreign Minister Richard Casey (1890-1976) declared in 1954 that: "We have every reason to want to live in harmony with our largest and closest neighbour" (cited in Woolcott 2003: 120). It might be said that: "Relations between Indonesia and Australia are too precious to be left to the whims and moods of their leaders and politicians, but this is exactly what has happened..." (Bayuni 2018: 304). There is only one thing worse: not having regular contact between the political class and leadership of both countries.

Whitlam in Opposition was a regular visitor to Indonesia. He thought that the relationship with Indonesia should be the centrepiece of Australian foreign policy engagement. On assumption of the ALP leadership, Whitlam wrote in *The Australian* newspaper that: "We are the only European people next to a large Asian nation" and that in contrast to the challenge: "...our aid to Indonesia... is trifling and ineffective" (*The Australian*, 18 February 1967). In government, Whitlam boasted: "Our civil aid... two and a half times the value of our defence aid – is an even more important element in our relations with Indonesia" (Whitlam 1973c: 340).

Whitlam with Indonesian President Soeharto in Jogjakarta in 1974. Photograph: National Archives of Australia.

Woolcott identifies why the focus on Indonesia is central to Australian strategic thinking:

> Indonesia's position as the largest and most politically complex of our neighbours, and its centrality to South-East Asia, mean that it must always be of major concern to Australia for geostrategic, political, economic, and social reasons. By any measure it is an important country but for Australia it is especially so, not least because of its potential to control much of our northern airspace and the sea lanes through which most of our export trade passes (Woolcott 2003: 120).

The notion of exotic difference can be exaggerated. Kelly noted: "Australia needs to see engagement as an intellectual and cultural exercise, and that demands a nation that is equipped with language and broader cultural skills to manage this challenge" (Kelly 2006: 36). Nearly all subsequent Australian prime ministers followed Whitlam's lead in making Indonesia the 'first port of call' on an overseas visit after obtaining leadership of Australia. At least three times when Whitlam was Opposition leader, he visited President Soeharto in Indonesia. Now as prime minister Whitlam visited Jakarta in 1973 and 1974 – and the two leaders forged a close relationship. Whitlam hosted President Soeharto in Townsville in 1975, which would prove to be the President's last visit to Australia. Closer Australian-Indonesian relations were "truncated by Indonesia's military incorporation of East Timor in 1975" (MacIntyre 1991: 145).

Having now discussed some of the major challenges faced by Whitlam, relevant to the conduct of Whitlam's foreign policy, is a brief discussion on his travels in pursuit of his objectives.

An Issue of Neutral Significance

Trips

Whitlam set a pattern for Australian leaders travelling extensively, as a means of developing rapport with other leaders. This was a soft projection of Australian influence, an opportunity to listen and gather intelligence, and a means to pursue Australian interests.

Since Whitlam, Australian prime ministers have travelled far more extensively, to more places, particularly in the Asian region, than was the pattern previously. Whitlam's travel pace, however, did not find universal favour. J.B. Paul complained of the PM's "forays, his posturing and his peregrinations as Foreign Minister" (Paul 1973a: 104). Then Opposition Leader, Billy Snedden, said: "... most people in Australia [say] that we would have our reputation more enhanced if the Prime Minister stayed here and did not go overseas with a giant *caravanserai* which pays tribute to him" (House of Representatives, *Hansard*, 5 December 1974, p. 4690). The controversy was about to get worse, because Cyclone Tracy in Christmas 1974 hit Darwin and wiped out much of the city's infrastructure and housing. After that Christmas, Whitlam hurriedly and briefly returned to Australia from a European tour, but Whitlam, the Philhellene, returned to Europe in the early New Year (1975).

Whitlam in Darwin after Cyclone Tracy struck. He had cut short his holiday in Europe, visited the Northern Territory, and returned to Greece a few days later. Photo: News Limited.

In February 1975, Whitlam said: "I stress ... [a] Prime Minister... has a special and at times an overriding duty to promote Australia's place in the world" (Whitlam 1975a: 61). John Menadue, recalled: "He loved travel... [I] pleaded with him not to go back overseas (to Greece & Rome [in early 1975, but he responded]): 'Comrade, if I am going to put up with the fuckwits in the Labor Party, I have got to have my trips'." (Menadue 1999: 135; almost the same words, Menadue 2020). Menadue, however, urges that: "The trips were never junkets; they recharged his spirits and refreshed his mind" (Menadue 1999: 134). Further, as Whitlam said: "Only a visit by a head of government enables Australia to put her point of view at the highest level and in the most forceful terms. Only a visit by a head of government obliges the countries visited to clarify and co-ordinate their policies towards us" (Whitlam 1975a: 61).

Perhaps, to momentarily play Devil's Advocate, those visits were not insignificant. They were symbolic, but they are appropriate to mention because they indicated unprecedented Australian engagement with the international community. Not for the first time, J.B. Paul got this wrong and Billy Snedden did too. John Menadue was no doubt correct about the domestic 'optics', but Whitlam was surely right about the benefits of travel to Australia as well as his own well-being. Even though the media looks for opportunities to criticise overseas holidays at taxpayers' expense – as was said about Scott Morrison's Hawaiian vacation in December 2019 in the midst of bad bushfires on the Australian east coast, and about Whitlam's return to Europe post-Cyclone Tracy. Whitlam changed Australian attitudes. Menadue was right: they are almost never junkets. Nobody would dare level such criticisms at a Prime Minister for extensive travel on government business these days.

Now to four areas that have elicited controversy and criticism – Vietnam, Timor, the recognition of the Baltic States, and government stances relating to the Middle East.

CONTROVERSIES

Vietnam

In the 1960s, Whitlam tried to balance support for the US alliance with opposition to extreme non-alignment and left-wing sentiment.

On Vietnam, some context is important. In April 1965 Prime Minister Menzies announced the Australian government's troop commitments to Vietnam. Ahead of that decision, in November 1964, he introduced a scheme of national service designed to create an army of 40,000 full-time soldiers. The internal divisions in America over the war eventually became seismic and had Australian echoes. The loss of blood and treasure, the interminability of the war, and uncertainty about America's commitment, meant that "during 1967 the war began to look more and more like a dubious and doomed enterprise." And Vietnam "induced the first shadow of unpopularity over the American connection in Australian public opinion" (Bell 1988b: 141). Conscription became a huge negative for Australians' support of the war (Bilney 2013: 274).

Labor's position in the latter 1960s shifted from withdrawal of conscripts and consultation with allies about what would happen next, to a harder position – total withdrawal and scepticism about involvement in what was frequently, if simplistically, called a civil war (K.C. Beazley 1983). Arthur Calwell's anti-war speech of 1965 canvassed the issues:

> We believe that America must not be humiliated and must not be forced to withdraw. But we are convinced that sooner or later the dispute in Vietnam must be settled through the councils of the United Nations. If it is necessary to back with a peace force the authority of the United Nations, we would support Australian participation to the hilt. But we believe that the military involvement in the present form decided on by the Australian Government represents a threat to Australia's standing in Asia, to our power for good in Asia and above all to the security of this nation (Calwell 1965; reprinted in Bramston 2113a :321-324; Fullilove 2005: 204-211; Kemp & Stanton 2004: 173-176).

Conscription was particularly divisive. In 1971, the McMahon Liberal-Country Party Coalition government announced the withdrawal of Australian combat troops by Christmas 1971, and the conscription period was reduced from two-years to 18-months. In government, Whitlam sought to shift Australia away from military interventions as the focus of policy: "Isolationism is not an option for Australia... We shall, for example, be giving even more economic aid to South Vietnam in the coming year than the previous government did in the last" (Whitlam 1973c: 338). But as Saigon was beginning to fall in April 1975, the Prime Minister dismissed concerns: "Who rules in Saigon is not, and never has been, an ingredient in Australia's security. Our strength, our security, rest on factors and relationships ultimately unchanged by these events." He went on:

> The really important factors and relations are... our relations

with our closest and largest neighbour, Indonesia; our relations with our greatest trading partner, Japan; our relations with China; our active support for the development of cooperation between the members of the Association of South East Asian Nations; our efforts to ensure that the Indian Ocean does not become the next area of confrontation between the superpowers as Indo-China became, in a sense, the first. Above all, Australia's security, as with the peace of the world, rests ultimately upon making the détente between the United States and the Soviet Union a success and upon associating China in a wider détente. These are the great relationships and the great factors which determine the security of Australia. (House of Representatives, *Hansard*, No. 15, 8 April 1975, p. 1260; partly quoted, Freudenberg 1993: 208).

A few years earlier, a pithy summary of Whitlam's wrestling with the demons of policy, the requirements of realism, and avoiding capricious policy change, came in this assessment: "Mr Whitlam genuinely abominated the Vietnam war in which he saw the United States playing out a monstrous role of oppression and intervention in a daily betrayal of traditional American ideals." That author went on:

> It is apparent that he still sees it the same way and cannot even concede that it might have been a mistaken crusade involving the expenditure of huge amounts of American blood and treasure or that, whatever it might have been, it gave needed time to other countries of the area to build stronger societies through their protection, at a particularly vulnerable time, from the side effects of North Vietnam's ferocious nationalism (Hastings 1973: 6).

This is an interesting statement capturing the dynamic pressures involved in conducting Australian policy.

Singapore's leader, Lee Kuan Yew (1923-2015) thought that American intervention enabled the newly minted, post-colonial governments in south-east Asia, to find their feet: "Although American intervention failed in Vietnam, it bought time for the rest of Southeast Asia" (Lee 2000: 457).

Whitlam is greeted by Singaporean Prime Minister Lee Kuan Yew in Singapore in 1974. Photograph: United Press International.

As Saigon was falling (4 March to 30 April 1975) on 8 April 1975, Whitlam told parliament: "While the security of Australia has never rested solely upon the American alliance, that alliance remains a key element in it. And whatever the outcome of the events now unfolding in Vietnam, the basic elements of Australia's security remain untouched" (House of Representatives, *Hansard*, No. 15, 8 April 1975, p. 1260; also, Freudenberg 1993: 208). As the South Vietnamese regime began to collapse: "In April 1975, with the fall of Saigon imminent,

Willesee was much troubled by the fate of those who might be identified with the former South Vietnamese regime." To Whitlam's annoyance. "[Willesee] made a determined attempt to convince Whitlam that Vietnamese wishing to enter Australia should not be subject to the restrictions applicable to other migrants, recommending in particular that asylum should be given to Vietnamese employed by the Australian Embassy." But "Whitlam was not persuaded" (Oliver 2010: 482). Because of Whitlam's intransigence concerning accepting a reasonable quota of refugees, Singapore's Lee said: "I was prepared to expose his moves and show him up as a sham white Afro-Asian" (Lee 2000: 395). Arguably, Whitlam adroitly 'managed' Vietnam policy until thousands of boats, laden with their frightened human cargo, pushed out to sea to escape northern rule and political and religious persecution.

Worth noting, though, is Freudenberg's spirited defence of Whitlam's handling of the collapse of South Vietnam and the consequent humanitarian crisis (Freudenberg 1977: 327-341). Former Whitlam minister Clyde Cameron (1913-2008) claimed Whitlam said to him that he did not want any "Vietnamese Balts coming into Australia" (Cameron 1990: 801). But those words were recorded in a diary entry dated Sunday 27 November 1977, recollecting what Whitlam allegedly said in April 1975. Whether or not such a brutal line was ever used by Whitlam, when Vietnamese refugees were pouring out of the country, he was not generous towards them (Viviani 1984: 53-115). Menadue regarded the handling of East Timor and treatment of Vietnamese refugees as the low points of Whitlam's prime ministership (Menadue 1999: 134).

Timor

There are few more fraught episodes in Australian foreign policy than the who-knew-what, who-acquiesced-to-what, what-should-have-happened controversy about East Timor in 1975 and beyond.

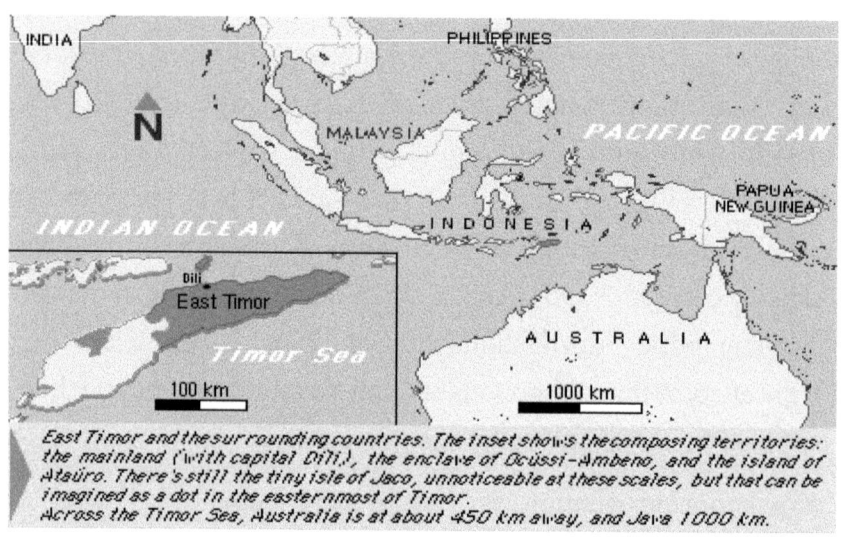

Map showing East Timor and proximity to Indonesia and Australia. Western Timor is part of Indonesia, part of the former Dutch West Indies. Across the East Timor Sea, 450km away, is Australia; Java is 1000km away. Image: https://etan.org/timor/1whitepg.htm, accessed 27 January 2023.

Portugal's 'Carnation Revolution' in 1974-75 saw a popular uprising against the dictatorship which had ruled since 1926, and an unravelling of relations with the administration of the country's colonies. These carnations had thorns. Mozambique, Angola, and other colonies declared independence with Marxist leaders rising to the top. Cuban military forces and mercenaries (in 'Operation Carlotta') came to support them in ensuing civil wars. In August 1975, the Portuguese Governor fled Timor, carelessly leaving behind weapons which were captured by the Revolutionary Front for an Independent East Timor (Portuguese: *Frente Revolucionária de Timor-Leste Independente*, abbreviated as Fretilin), the radical pro-Marxist wing of the independence movement. Civil war broke out, including with pro-Indonesian allies. Any Australian government faced an unappetising "dilemma" (Adams 1976: 125-126) or, rather, a series of them.

Quoting from the diplomatic cables of Richard ("Dick") Woolcott, Walsh and Munster provide a timeline and evidence about Whitlam views. On 15 September 1974 in Jogjakarta Whitlam spoked with President Soeharto, expressing the opinion that an independent Timor was not viable. On 3-5 April 1975, they met again in Townsville, but what was said between them remains murky (Walsh & Munster 1980: 186-188; incidentally, their book was temporarily banned – Walsh and Munster 1982). Whitlam comments on that meeting: "We were frustrated ... by the irresponsibility of the Portuguese and the intransigence of the Timorese parties" (Whitlam 1985: 108).

Curiously and controversially, Hocking's biography argues that he-knew-he-shouldn't-so-he-didn't:

> The Whitlam government's overarching policy on Portuguese Timor was simple and consistent: self-determination, the form of which to be decided by an 'internationally recognised' expression of the will of the people. The very notion of enforced incorporation ... was completely at odds with Whitlam's fundamental commitment to ending colonialism, and with Labor Party policy (Hocking 2012: 379).

Ahuh. More bluntly, Foreign Minister "Willesee believed Australia should try to persuade Indonesia to accept an independent East Timor and was troubled that Australia might be seen as complicit in any military action by Indonesia." So seriously did he regard the situation that: "In August 1975 he wrote to the Prime Minister arguing that if the Australian Government, having been forewarned of Indonesian military intervention, failed to state its views clearly, it would be placed in an 'embarrassing and politically indefensible position'" (Oliver 2010: 483).

On 16 October 1975, five Australian journalists covering the unrest were killed in the town of Balibo, apparently by Indonesian troops who were "secretly" in the territory in support of their proxies in East Timor. Whitlam was out of office (dismissed by the Governor General on 11 November 1975) when Indonesia invaded on 7 December (Freudenberg 1993: 207), six days before the Australian election. On 6 December "President Gerald Ford and Secretary of State Kissinger were in Jakarta" (Menadue 1999: 134). "Whitlam believed that the Indonesian invasion of East Timor would not have taken place had he remained in office" (Hocking: 385). Yet, when in office he had said: "I am in favour of incorporation, but obeisance has to be made to self-determination" (Gyngell 2017: 117). Ambivalence can have drawbacks and permissive consequence.

There is an extensive, critical literature alleging that the Whitlam government and the Fraser government (caretaker, from 11 November, then onwards to 1983 after the election of 13 December 1975), downplayed the human catastrophe occurring in East Timor (Job 2021). Watson describes the tiny, former Portuguese colony as "forgotten", as if oblivious to the ongoing controversies domestically in Australia from 1975. In Whitlam, Watson contrasts the self-image of an erudite social democrat with the person allegedly and culpably involved in Indonesia's invasion. Watson analyses developments in the context of decolonisation, Portugal's domestic upheavals, the Cold War, regional security, and Australia's quest to find a new role in Asia. He claims that Australian leaders' 'greenlighting' of Soeharto was an exercise in *realpolitik* (Watson 2021). This is not as weak as it sounds as, "... on the basis of a realpolitik analysis, there was clearly logic in Whitlam's policy" (Bell 1988b: 126). Whitlam was also true to his earlier position on the incorporation of Irian Jaya as part of Indonesia.

Whitlam was unsympathetic to claims for East Timor independence, its pretensions to economic and security viability, and he seemed accepting of Indonesia's takeover. Whitlam had in mind the colonial legacy. Amongst the Europeans, the Portuguese were second worst to the Belgians in their woeful management and lack of application to the social and economic development of their possessions. They left little behind. How could any Timor state survive?

Whitlam probably knew General Soeharto would strike and seize East Timor. Kim Beazley Snr. thought: "Whitlam believed in a world uncluttered by minor powers" (K.E. Beazley 2009: 225). Viviani, partly in sympathetic regret, said: "It was Indonesia that was the centrepiece of Whitlam's Asia policy, and Indonesia in the end that cost Whitlam most in his foreign policy record" (Viviani 1997: 106).

Baltic States

Whitlam, in his capacity as Acting Foreign Minister, endorsed a recommendation from Alan Renouf (1919-2008), the Secretary of the Department of Foreign Affairs, 1974-77, that in support of détente, Australia should change from *de facto* to *de jure* recognition of Soviet sovereignty over the Baltic states of Latvia, Lithuania and Estonia (Bilney 2013: 278; Freudenberg 1993). Why did Australia recognise Soviet *de jure* incorporation? What was in it for world order? What was in it for Australia? His minister, Don Willesee, then overseas in South America, was not consulted. Yet on August 13, 1974, the Foreign Affairs Minister thought he himself should announce in the Senate that in the previous month the government had decided "to accord *de jure* recognition of the incorporation of the Baltic States into the Soviet Union" (*Senate Debates*, 13 August 1974, pp. 781-2). "Publicly, he endorsed the decision while, privately, he regarded it as hasty and politically inept" (Oliver 2010: 481). This was one of the strangest decisions in Whitlam's time, as "no domestic political grouping was campaigning for this recognition..." (Suter 1975: 73).

Were there trade considerations? Apparently not. In March 1973, the government hosted Nikolai Patolichev (1908-1989), the USSR's minister for foreign trade (Whitlam 1973c: 337). But on that visit, there was no pressing of Australia for diplomatic gestures.

With the *de jure* decision in 1974, the Opposition condemned "the unseemly readiness to co-operate with the Soviet Union over the Baltic States" (Peacock 1974). There appeared no quid pro quo from the Soviets for Whitlam's gesture. A reason why might be apparent from this admittedly relayed account of Whitlam's visit to the Soviet Union in January 1975. According to the Rev. Fr. Frank Brennan, the Special Minister for State, Lionel Bowen (1922-2012) a great mimic of "Gough", joined Whitlam on this leg of Whitlam's journey through Europe. John Faulkner, NSW Labor Senator 1989-2015, told Brennan what Bowen said:

> ... [A]long with Gough, [Lionel] met with Alexei Kosygin and other Soviet leaders. The meeting dragged. With the aid of a translator, apparently Kosygin said "I'm delighted to have this meeting. This is the first occasion an Australian Prime Minister has visited the Kremlin despite the fact we have fought alongside each other in two world wars. Now, let's do something big to honour this occasion, like a major trade announcement. The Soviet Union could take a substantial amount of your wheat and your wool, and you, from Australia, could reciprocate with landing rights for Aeroflot, and take minerals and cargo ships from the Soviet Union." Gough responded, I am told, to a speechless Kosygin and certainly a stunned Lionel Bowen: "I don't want to talk with you about mundane things like trade. I want to know what happened to the Grand Duchess Anastasia in 1918" (Brennan 2017).

There was no trade announcement that year.

But there was the signing of an agreement on scientific, technical and cultural collaboration during that visit. Whitlam's account refers to his arrival on 12 January 1975 and two days later to Moscow "where I had wide-ranging discussions with President Podgorny and Prime Minister Kosygin of the Soviet Union and signed cultural and scientific agreements between the Soviet Union and Australia" (Whitlam 1975a: 63). In conclusion,

Gough Whitlam and the Soviet Premier, Alexei Kosygin, sign an agreement in Moscow, 1975 on scientific, technical, and cultural collaboration. Photograph: Express Newspapers/Hulton Archive.

the acceptance by Whitlam of Renouf's advice conferred no advantages and only received backlash in Australia. It was bizarre and unnecessary. Seventeen years later, the Soviet Union was "kaput".

The Middle East

Whitlam advocated an 'even handed' approach to what was then known as 'the Arab-Israel conflict' in the Middle East. He had met every Labour Prime Minister of Israel (Whitlam 1985: 124). In Opposition, he visited the Jewish state five times: in 1964, shortly after the war in September 1967, in December 1968, in December 1971, and June 1976 (Whitlam 1985: 124-125; Mendes 2023; Rutland 2012: 40). Prior to winning election in

1972, Whitlam was seen as a strong supporter of Israel, praising its democracy, and even urging that Qantas investigate flight routes from Australia (Mendes 2023). During Whitlam's prime ministership, Australia opened a Trade Office in Tel Aviv (Rutland 2012: 40). In a statement in February 1975, he said: "In my discussions on the Middle East I asserted the right of all countries in the Middle East including Israel, to secure and recognised boundaries. I believe that Israel's integrity as a state must be upheld. At the same time, a lasting solution in the Middle East will require withdrawal from occupied territories and measures to meet the legitimate needs of the Palestinian people" (Whitlam 1975a: 64). This was a consistently articulated position. This version of even handedness was broadly uncontroversial within Australia, and a bi-partisan position (Albinski 1977: 135-143).

Whitlam's memoirs reference his visits to the Lebanon in 1968 and 1971 when: "I became increasingly aware of the sufferings of the Palestinian people and the attitudes of the other Arab nations" (Whitlam 1985: 124). On his fifth visit, as Opposition Leader in June 1976, he met Prime Minister Yitzhak Rabin. Whitlam observed that: "Australian diplomats have to live with the fact that the Arab and Islamic nations will not support the US when it is thought to condone Israel's disregard of human rights and defiance of the UN in the occupied territories" (Whitlam 1985: 126). His memoirs express a harsher characterisation of the Israel/Palestinian situation than what he had expressed as prime minister.

Some sections of the ALP, mostly within the Victorian Labor Unity faction, plus the organised Jewish community argued that Whitlam's position was unbalanced and antipathetic to Israel. Perhaps, however, Whitlam saw himself as striking a middle ground between contending views.

Then ACTU President Bob Hawke visiting Israeli Prime Minister Golda Meir in 1971, on his first visit to Israel. Photo: *Australian Jewish News*.

In November 1973, future Australian Prime Minister, and then Australian Council of Trade Unions President Bob Hawke told US diplomats that he found Whitlam's approach to Israel and Middle East issues "beyond belief". Hawke was especially critical of what he called Mr Whitlam's "immoral, unethical and ungrateful" attitude towards Israel (Dorling 2013). According to cables leaked by Wikileaks in 2013, based on 11,000 cables from the US embassy in Canberra and its consulates in Sydney and Melbourne, Hawke talked at the time about "Whitlam's 'unprintable' even-handed 'unprintable' Arab policy". The cables indicate Hawke thought Whitlam had "caved in" to the Arab side in the Middle East for "commercial reasons". This refers to when the major OPEC – including Arab – 'oil' nations hiked petroleum prices after the 6-25 October 1973 Yom Kippur War, coinciding with Whitlam's pronouncements about Canberra's "even-handed" policy towards Israel and the Arab world.

Hawke lamented that although Whitlam promised he would be the first Australian PM to visit Israel, "…he never got closer than Rhodes" (Kohn 2013). Reich, in a survey of Australian policy towards Israel in the early 1970s, saw Whitlam as unsympathetic to Israel. (Reich 2010). Undoubtedly, after the June 1967 Six Day war, many on the left drifted from warmth to harsh criticism of Israel, with the "occupation" of the West Bank in mind. Prior to then, as Mendes says: "…the global left was relatively sympathetic to the State of Israel" (Mendes 2023). Published months after victory in that conflict, however, maverick Jewish intellectual Frank Knopfelmacher predicted: "In losing their status as victims, as objects of patronizing generosity, the Jews will lose their status as pets of the Left… In the eyes of the masochistic Left they have, furthermore, also committed the most unpardonable of crimes – they have won…" (Knopfelmacher 1967: 64). Knopfelmacher had in mind some of the more extreme figures on the Left. Writing in the early 1980s, the sociologist and political scientist Professor Sol Encel (1925-2010), himself politically progressive, close to the ALP, and active in the Jewish community, remarked in his survey of opinion in the ALP: "Much of this left-wing hostility emanates from groups outside of the ALP. It has, however, surfaced within the ALP itself, most notably among members of the Socialist Left faction within the party in Victoria" (Encel 2004: 58). Knopfelmacher estimated: "It would be wrong to assume that the change in Jewish political alignments will be rapid, or that the process will be smooth, or that its consequences will be uniformly good or desirable" (Knopfelmacher 1967: 64).

Hawke and others saw Whitlam as *emotionally* disengaged from the story of Israel and the vulnerability of the Jewish people in the Middle East. This came to a head during the Yom Kippur War when Israel's very existence was literally under attack by Egypt, Syria, and a coalition of Arab states. The war resulted in the deaths of 2,688 Israeli soldiers and 7,250 wounded. (Rutland 2021: 236). In October 1973 Hawke wanted Whitlam to express empathy, sympathy, solidarity, with Israel rather than steely-eyed non-partisanship. In November 1973, Hawke was the first non-Israeli to visit the Golan Heights after the war, to see battle zones, death, and carnage (Bramston 2022: 178). Hawke thought that the agency of the UN in resolving conflicts was impossible, given the U.N. member states' hostility to Israel. In Knopfelmacher's colourful description:

> For the time being, the U.N. continues to act as a stage for a curious schizophrenic farce. The projected victim of annihilation who had the temerity to survive is treated to stern moral reprimands by the unsuccessful bullies. Such residues of reality which occasionally penetrated U.N. debates in the past have been abandoned, and the world is treated to purely psychotic transactions which can no longer be regarded even as propaganda with some claim to credibility. (Knopfelmacher 1967: 57).

Worse was to come in U.N. fora.

In July 1975, at the first International Women's Conference in Mexico City, Australia voted for a resolution which stated: "Women, as well as men, should eliminate colonialism, neo-colonialism, foreign domination and occupation, Zionism, apartheid [and racial discrimination." (Rutland 2012: 43). This presaged the notorious 10 November 1975 U.N. General Assembly Resolution 3379 (XXX), which declared that "Zionism is a form of racism and racial discrimination."

As earlier noted, two of Whitlam's senior advisers, Wilenski and Spigelman, were Jewish, from families deeply affected by the horrors of the Shoah. They were supporters of Israel's right to exist and would never countenance open hostility, notwithstanding any personal misgivings about particular Israeli policies and actions. Sometimes Graham Freudenberg is added as the third prominent Jewish adviser to Whitlam in government (Kemp 2022: 149); but he was not Jewish. In this author's view, the influence of Wilenski and Spigelman as senior public servants appointed by Whitlam means that the claim that Whitlam was anti-Israel is too simplistic. Admittedly, however, I cannot source evidence that Spigelman and Wilenski, as Jews, influenced or sought to influence Whitlam's position on Israel. No doubt, Whitlam took advice from a range of sources including the different factions within the parliamentary party, and foreign policy advisors and diplomats – many of whom, judging from Reich's 2010 research – seem to have been "pro-Arab". Additionally, Whitlam stated in his memoirs he was influenced by the increasing numbers of Arabs voting in key electorates.

Notwithstanding the general position of officials in the

Department of Foreign Affairs evincing scepticism to hostility to Australia's raising this issue (Rutland 2014), in Moscow in January 1975, Whitlam met Prime Minister Kosygin and made a presentation on the question of Jewish emigration from the Soviet Union (AJN, 16 January 1975: 1): "No purpose is served if we avoid issues where agreement is unlikely. The Soviet Union has a better understanding of our views and, I believe, a greater respect for our candour" (Whitlam 1975a: 66). Yet later in the year, Whitlam's canvassing for an election campaign donation from Saddam Hussein's Iraqi Ba'ath Socialist Party', as discussed below in the next section of this monograph, forever soured relations with much of the Australian Jewish community (Dorling 2011). Relations were already curdled, as discussed below, for multiple reasons. There was the lingering anger around the government's inaction to support Israel during the Yom Kippur War. On the Ba'ath controversy, a long-time friend of Whitlam, Syd Einfeld (1909-1996; Federal MP for Phillip, 1961-63; NSW State MP, 1965-84), a respected Labor figure prominent in the Australian Jewish community, proclaimed: "I disown such an idea, if it is true, and I believe that Labor Party participants in that sort of a deal and plan should be expelled from the party forthwith" (AJN, 4 March 1976: 3). This, necessarily, included Whitlam.

As bad as that episode was, and notwithstanding lapses of judgement and expression, I contend that Whitlam's policy and actions *in government* set a bi-partisan benchmark, including support for a two-state solution, that all subsequent governments have followed. In his memoirs, Whitlam argued that this was part of his legacy (Whitlam 1985: 738).

Encel however, observed that some leading members of the Jewish community recommended that Jews not vote Labor in December 1975, "...the only occasion when such action has been taken. These events represent the nadir of relationships between the Jewish community and the Labor Party" (Encel 2004: 59). Though, a few days before the election, the *Australian Jewish News* editorialised that: "Leaders of the organised community have stated on a number of occasions — and we fully adopted the principle — that there will be no communal stand for or against the policies of any major party" (AJN, 11 December 1975: 2). Yet animosity from key communal leaders was intense.

The main reasons for this were dissatisfaction with Whitlam's biased, 'tilted hand' position during the Yom Kippur War and otherwise; certain votes by Australia in international fora; and occasionally Whitlam's demeanour in dealing with the community. On the former, Hawke claimed in January 1974 that even handedness was: "Morally repugnant and inconsistent with ALP policy, which required the Arab states to recognise Israel's sovereignty and right to exist…" (Hawke 1994: 78). At different times, Labor figures including Hawke, Barry Cohen MP, Richard ("Dick") Klugman MP, Dr Moss Cass MP, Joe Berinson MP, Joan Child MP, Joe Riordan MP, Clyde Holding MP, and South Australian Labor Premier Don Dunstan and Einfield, urged Whitlam to be more publicly supportive of Israel (Rutland 2012: 55-56; Mendes 2023). For example, in October 1973, after Egyptian tanks crossed the Suez Canal on their way to attacking Israel, Cass urged Whitlam to call for a cease-fire. Whitlam refused. But Whitlam did call for a cease-fire as Israel was winning (Encel 2004: 58).

With respect to Australia's position on certain international and U.N. resolutions, in April 1973, Australia voted in favour of condemning Israel's retaliation against the PLO in the Lebanon for its attack on an Israeli township in northern Israel. The resolution did not condemn the PLO for initiating this conflagration (Rutland 2012: 53). Australia, in November 1974, abstained from voting against the resolution to expel Israel from the UNESCO European Regional Group, whereas most western European counties voted against. In June 1975, in Geneva at the International Labour Organization, the Australian government voted to admit the PLO as an observer, despite the ACTU and the Australian employers delegations voting against. The latter delegations wanted the PLO to recognise Israel's right to exist before agreeing. (Rutland 2012: 42-44). As mentioned above, in July 1975 there was the International Women's Conference vote condemning Zionism.

At a meeting with Jewish communal figures in April 1974 at the Chevron Hotel in Melbourne, an exasperated Whitlam snapped: "You people are difficult to please" (Rutland 2021: 213-219; Rutland 2012: 57; Encel 2004: 58). This thoughtless remark understandably inflamed passions. In the aftermath, *Melbourne Age* commentator Creighton Burns argued that sometimes Whitlam's demeanour, arrogance, sense of superiority, detracted from his otherwise reasonable perspective: That Israel should be recognised by its adversaries, including the PLO, as having the right to exist behind secure and recognised boundaries; and that support for a two-state solution including the formation of a Palestinian entity, should be Australian policy. (Burns 1974).

Whitlam was mostly disciplined in his approach to Israel and usually sought to follow the political line adopted by the Israeli Labour Party. This gave rise to two issues. First, Whitlam appreciated the Israel position from a NSW perspective, in which the Jewish community locally also mostly followed the Israeli Labour Party line. Victoria was much more hard-line and much more vocal in its criticism. Whitlam was then criticised by the Victorian Jewish community, which was influential in the Hawke position.

Second, unusually for Whitlam, his use of language sometimes let him down. Whitlam was an old-fashioned liberal intellectual; his knowledge and use of language was superb; but he naively believed that the substance of an argument was the essence of issues (a common error for lawyers), when, in international affairs, much nuance inheres in language. Thus, he used the term "the legitimate rights of the Palestinian people" which internationally carried with it a particular meaning that included statehood and issues around Jerusalem. This raised the ire of the Victorian Jewish community in particular. Ironically, in using the term "secure borders" as a right for Israel, he also alienated many in the Palestinian cause, because that phrase, similarly, carried with it an implied acceptance of some Israeli territorial claims associated with the Golan Heights and the West Bank.

Whitlam's declarations concerning the Middle East were sometimes coldly indifferent to the plight of the one democracy in the region, particularly during the 1973 Yom Kippur War. Whitlam's critique of Israel, without a similar critique of the Palestinians and the Arab world was highly problematic. The 'even handedness' approach should not mean the dictatorship of relativism by excusing one wrong by straining to see bad on the other 'side' at the same time. Whitlam the person fell short of the principled policy position he was supposedly standing by. A fair judgement, however, is that all Australian governments before and since, with greater finesse, have advocated substantially similar policies on Israel's right to exist, the need for a Palestinian settlement, and a two-state solution.

And now to an episode of troubling consequence in assessing Whitlam's judgement.

Iraqi Ba'ath Socialist Party Loan Affair

Arguably the most disturbing episode in Whitlam's political career is the secret effort to procure an AUD$500,000 donation from the Iraqi Ba'ath Socialist Party to fund Labor's election campaign in 1975. The 11 November 1975 dismissal caught Labor by surprise, campaign funds were near empty and, given the controversial period of Labor-in-office, donations from business circles had vanished (Sexton 2005: 269). In late November 1975, national ALP secretary David Coombe (1943-2019) along with Victorian Labor luminary, hard socialist left ideologue, and former state secretary Bill Hartley (1930-2006) – soon to be forever known as "Baghdad Bill" – concocted the scheme and consulted with Whitlam (Oakes 1976: 270-295).

The money failed to materialise (Hocking 2012: 364). In March 1976, the ALP national executive condemned all three for their "grave errors of judgment" concerning the proposed gift for the 1975 election campaign (Reid 1976: 453). That came after Coombe and Whitlam in January 1976 falsely assured the ALP national executive that there were sufficient funds to meet the party's debts from the just concluded December 1975 election campaign. Whitlam 'owned up' after he was re-elected by the parliamentary party as leader – after Bill Hayden, the former Treasurer, declined to stand.

The bizarre story included a post-election breakfast meeting in McMahons Point attended by the Labor trio, a two-man delegation from the Iraqi Foreign Ministry – secret police chief and torturer Farouk Abdulla Yehya and Saddam relative Ghafil Jassim Al-Tikriti (Connor 2016: 36), and their shadowy intermediatory, Henry Fischer, an antisemite who had not long before edited a lunar right political journal. It is alleged that Fischer subsequently absconded with the Iraqi money he had raised for the ALP (Dorling).

The story is compellingly told in a chapter of Laurie Oakes' book *Crash Through or Crash* (1976). At one stage, according to the Oakes account, Hartley forwarded fund-raising letters to Iraq's Saddam Hussein and to Yasser Arafat, the head of the Palestine Liberation Organisation. As no funds were received, the ALP went into 'hock' to pay for the 1975 campaign debt. Rutland details memos and other material relating to the Australian-born retailer Reuben F. Scarf (1913-93), of Christian Lebanese descent who, through the Frank and Nahida Scarf Memorial Foundation, employed Fischer, and urged Whitlam to recognise the PLO and enable them to set up a diplomatic office in Australia (Rutland 2012: pp. 59-63).

The Iraqi loans affair is not strictly a matter of foreign policy, but legitimate questions arise as to whether this 'blood money' might have attracted a change in policy by Whitlam on Middle East issues. Had Whitlam won re-election in 1975, had the donation been received, and everything kept a secret, the consequences for Australian foreign policy are troubling. The secrecy of the deal exposed Whitlam to blackmail. Moreover, proximity to the "disastrous attempts by members of the Whitlam Cabinet to raise overseas loans in 1974 and 1975, demonstrated that, whatever his other qualities, Gough Whitlam was grossly deficient in the crucial area of political judgment" (Henderson 1990). The story came to light in early 1976. Hawke, in his memoirs wrote: "... that Whitlam, who was aware of the abhorrent nature of this regime, should acquiesce appalled me beyond measure" (Hawke 1994: 79).

At a University of NSW ALP Club meeting on 31 March 1976, I asked Whitlam-supporter and ALP Senator Jim McClelland (1915-99) about this affair. He looked down, sighed, and proffered that in the stress of the dismissal, for Whitlam to entertain this idea was a moment of insanity. McClelland exhorted that Whitlam should not be judged by that mistake alone. True. But it was more than a momentary lapse given the months from being first told, enthusiasm for the idea, and the coverup by Whitlam. Others were not as generous as McClelland. Kim E. Beazley resigned from the Federal Shadow Ministry: "I felt broken-hearted about Whitlam's leadership." (K.E. Beazley 2009: 239). Senator John Wheeldon (1929-2006) also resigned from Shadow Cabinet. In fairness to McClelland, in the aftermath, he urged that Hayden challenge Whitlam for the leadership of the party (Hayden 1996: 305). After I started work at the Labor Council of NSW, Lionel Bowen in 1978, told me that based on this episode he thought Whitlam had gone "mad".

Assessment

Consistency and innovation are intertwined in policy development. Goldsworthy saw the early years of the Whitlam government as carried by a determination "to act idealistically and more independently, without forfeiting the tangible benefits of old connections." (Goldsworthy 1974b). Whitlam said of his policy, eschewing the either/or nomenclature: "It is idealistic, yet realistic" (Whitlam 1973d: 14). Those words suggest a clue for appraising Whitlam's distinct, foreign policy positioning. Few theorists/practitioners are purely one or the other. As one of Whitlam's critics, the foreign policy analyst and commentator Owen Harries put the matter, the aim of foreign policy "...is not perfection – not utopian bliss – but decency. It is, more often than not, a morality of the lesser evil, of prudence" (Harries 2005 in Switzer & Windybank 2022: 18). As Harries elsewhere expressed the point:

> ...instead of classifying people as either wholly realist or wholly moral, it might be better to acknowledge both elements exist in most if not all of us, the nature of the mix depending partly on temperament, but also on experience and understanding of the facts of a particular situation, and the nature of the international system in general. (Harries 2009).

In this vein, Whitlam's views on the legal architecture of international human rights law, the potential place of the U.N. to assist resolving international conflict, place him in the idealist camp. Yet his attitudes to dealing with Indonesia and China, for example, might be characterised as realistic and pragmatic. Whitlam's actions and thinking were an untidy mix of perspectives, policy positions, and priorities.

An interesting case is the evolution of Whitlam's thinking on the Vietnam conflict, which shifted from opposition to Australian conscription, and criticism of the way the Americans fought the war, to a position that America should abandon the South Vietnamese, describing the North's win as: "Viet Nam's victory in her war of independence" (Whitlam 1981: 53.).

How big a splash did Whitlam make to policy? Hudson wrote that he was "struck much more by the continuities in Australia's foreign policies in changing circumstances and irrespective of parties in government than by radical changes." And he compared the zeal and a busyness of Labor under Whitlam to another energetic period in the 1950s under Casey (Hudson 1972: 119). Similarly, W. Macmahon Ball (1901-1986), diplomat, political scientist, gadfly, saw the Vietnam era, 1965-72, when Australian troops were committed, as an exceptional period, with broad consistency of policy otherwise. He argued the main differences were "mainly differences of style and emphasis. ... The Labor Party, as led by Mr Whitlam, tends to emphasise the other friends it is making, such as China and Third World countries, also knowing well that these new connections do not yet amount to much in the way of solid advantages..." (W.M. Ball 1974: 4). This is too sweepingly simplistic. The exception of Vietnam was major. Australian Labor tends to be much more independently minded than the Coalition in interpreting obligations and actions under the Australian-American alliance. (In more recent times, without dwelling on the merits, the example of the ALP's opposition in 2003 to Prime Minister Howard sending a modest contingent of military forces to the second Iraq war is a case in point.)

Whitlam, in contrast to the "continuity story" of Australian foreign policy, specialised in innovation. In a major statement to the parliament in May 1973 on 'Australia's Foreign Policy', he argued:

> Our work in the last 5 months has lain not in forcing new directions upon Australia's foreign policy but in making new definitions of the role of foreign policy. Australia's international relations, like those of any other country, must always be directed to maintaining the nation's security and integrity (Whitlam 1973c: 336).

He saw his work as complemented by:

> ...the pivotal role played by President Nixon in ushering in a new and saner phase in our relations with China; in clearing the way for more intensive commercial, scientific, technical and cultural exchanges between the United States of America and the Soviet Union, and thereby achieving a successful first round of the Strategic Arms Limitation Talks and ending foreign intervention in Vietnam (Whitlam 1973c: 336).

And then he summed up the direction of policy: "We must now view the conduct of external relations as a task which involves a total evaluation of our interests abroad and at home" (Whitlam 1973c: 336-337).

Peacock claimed there was the: "...pointless and inconsistent activism. ... The realities of international politics, which turn largely on the fact that relations are largely power relations and interests mainly national interests, are not particularly pleasant ones and any civilised man would wish them to be different." (Peacock 1974). Another opinion was: "In the Liberal view, it was by no means evident that great-power détente was yet a reality. Even if it were, the developing big-power condominium might actually limit rather than increase Australia's options..." (Goldsworthy 1974b: 112). Therefore, 'stick with your friends' was their simple view.

But Whitlam too saw the world as it is: "A generous foreign policy rests upon a proper balance between power and obligations. ... The aim ... is to develop foreign policies which are realistic and generous, enlightened yet pragmatic. 'Pragmatic' means in part a true recognition of the world as it is" (Whitlam 1973d: 3-4).

Foreign Minister Don Willesee, Prime Minister Gough Whitlam, and Dr Henry Kissinger in 1974. Photograph: The Australian Archives.

Whitlam took distinct positions on the US alliance that significantly impacted US attitudes, and while he insisted on more control over US engagement on Australian soil, he also contributed to a view on whether Australia and the ALP could be relied upon. Despite suspicions from some American policy makers, he helped to mostly settle the controversy within the ALP over what became more credibly known as the joint facilities. Whitlam and Barnard were right about this. Facilities like Pine Gap protect hosts (and potential aggressors) as well as the US. Without the intelligence gathered by such facilities, the US could be tempted to exercise first use. It could not afford to risk its assets if the Australian facilities were to be knocked out. The absence of those facilities would have endangered everyone. That is what the Labor Left at the time, especially in Victoria, failed to appreciate. On China, Whitlam envisaged symbiosis between Australia and China which relied on an independent Australia and a stable China, accepting of the US Alliance, so long as Australia independently assessed the issues with China. The recent history and the current relationship have significant echoes of the issues then discussed. Some of the first visits by senior Chinese leaders to "the West" were to Australia. For example, both Hu Yaobang as CCP General Secretary in 1985 and Zhao Ziyang, the then Premier, in 1983, made Australia the first western country they visited – a tribute to the close relations established in and after Whitlam's time. It is a worthy ambition to be a *zhengyou* — the true friend. As Prime Minister Rudd put matters in an address to Peking University students in 2008:

> A true friend is one who can be a "zhengyou", that is a partner

who sees beyond immediate benefit to the broader and firm basis for continuing, profound and sincere friendship ... a true friendship which "offers unflinching advice and counsels restraint" to engage in principled dialogue about matters of contention. It is the kind of friendship that I know is treasured in China's political tradition (Rudd 2008; for some Chinese reactions, Rudd 2018: 46-47).

That ought to be a continuing, prime objective, begun by Whitlam, pursued by subsequent Australian governments, notwithstanding the left adventurism of President Xi (J. Fitzgerald 2022; Rudd 2022: especially, 307-330).

Whitlam also held distinct views about Vietnamese refugees and East Timor that diminished his standing on human rights and people's right to self-determination. There is a striking contrast between Whitlam's stance on East Timor independence/the Baltic states from the traditional centre-left, social democratic support for national self-determination.

Whitlam certainly had boundless power over Australia's foreign policy. Being *prima donna assoluta* ("the dominant prima donna"), as he once jokingly said of himself, however, was sometimes a problem. Whitlam's brilliance in 1971, overruling Freudenberg's reservations (Oakes 1973: 216; Freudenberg 1977: 203), in deciding to go to China, made Whitlam think he could do anything. If he had of better consulted with Willesee, also with close figures in his Cabinet, even his ministry, some mistakes might have been avoided or mitigated. As Beazley once frustratedly murmured: "Gough, I have no fear of anything except your masterstrokes; they never work" (K.E. Beazley 2009: 224). In politics and foreign policy-making hubris can be the partner of the bold and creative. There is merit in the assessment of the Australian diplomatic and military historian, Peter Edwards: "Whitlam's tight personal hold on foreign policy wasn't always wise... Senator Don Willesee was no visionary, but he had sound political instincts and a sense of decency that complemented Whitlam's qualities" (Edwards 2016).

Whitlam made a difference to Australia's future. First, he attractively advocated Australia's place in the world in the context of a realistic, yet principled, outlook. Second, he disputed and urged Australians to discard the dread and fear that the country is trapped on the outside of an incomprehensible Asia. Third, he moved away from the quagmire of Vietnam and the military-dominant mindset of foreign policy. Fourth, he decisively shifted Australian sensitivities to engender better relations with Asian nations, particularly Indonesia.

Whitlamism was greater than the man. This is one counter to the hysterical reflection by a recent, former Liberal Cabinet minister who, to the question 'was Whitlam a great man?' responded: "...undoubtedly the answer is 'yes', in the way the world pays that dubious compliment to important historical figures without overmuch moral fussiness, averting its eyes from a multitude of sins" (Brandis 2022). Mistakes, there were many, achievements, at least as much. To compare Whitlam to some historical monster on the world stage, as this formulation suggests, is absurd.

Whatever Whitlam's triumphs, insights, daring, flaws, mistakes, naivety, myopia, he asked the portentous questions and inspired a democratic, idealistic realism. His promise was to address questions and priorities about the national interest, national security, identity, and national destiny, as well as he could. Critics of Whitlam rarely understood that his appeal lay in how he perceived the world and what he confidently proclaimed about what should and could be. In that pragmatic worldview, particularly on the international stage, there was nobility of purpose. In politics, foreign policy included, nobody gets everything they want. That is frustrating, especially when ideologues and opportunists swarm to absolutist positions.

The alternative is the approach contained in Whitlamism – seeking to do good while advancing the national interest. In doing so, results matter: "Important as it is to know the truth and to respond relevantly and steadfastly to it, the test of action is in the results" (Acheson 1970: 728). Continuing Acheson's metaphor cited at the beginning of this monograph about the foreign policy doer as gardener who must "use the forces of life, growth and nature, to his purpose", in this monograph we can see results of Whitlam's efforts. Some seeds fall on stony places, some fall among thorns, some struggle to take root. The fruits successfully harvested, those unpicked, and those that fell on barren ground, are described, analysed, and enable a fresh appraisal.

Author's Postscript

I am grateful to readers who critiqued an earlier draft, (Easson 2022) and subsequent iterations, including Kim C. Beazley, Michaela Browning, David Clune, Michael Costello, Shane Easson, Damian Grace, Catherine Harding, Tommy Koh, Philip Mendes, Scott Prasser, Stephen Rothman, Suzanne Rutland, Tom Switzer, and Susan Windybank. All errors and omissions are mine alone.

Compared to the shorter version of this paper, I have added detail and colour here and there to aspects of the story. I shifted the debate on the Middle East to the section on 'Controversies'. The more I delved into that area, the more complicated was any reasonable conclusion. This discussion also fitted better as immediately before the account of the Iraqi party loans controversy. So re-ordering was sensible, even if the discussion on that region is longer than, say, the account of Whitlam's China initiatives.

Perhaps it is an ironic tribute to Whitlam's success there, notwithstanding current controversies about Australia's relationship with China, that the opening of diplomatic ties in 1972 is now seen as necessary and relatively uncontroversial. Whitlam's move in 1971 to visit China and forge diplomatic links, was innovative and courageous. This was in defiance of conservative allegations that Whitlam was soft on communism, a witless tool of Mao, and conducting – in Prime Minister McMahon's phrase – "instant coffee" diplomacy (Fitzgerald 1972: 32). It is not unfair to say that Coalition governments in the early 1970s were lazy and confused or, more charitably, unable to guide a small power at sea in a storm – as UNSW Politics academic, a political conservative, Tony Palfreeman once told his students in the early 1970s. Even Owen Harries in 1972, despite then being an unapologetic Cold War Warrior and supporter of South Vietnam, remarked to Whitlam in a television studio that as he was so dismayed at the disarray of the Liberal government that he would vote Labor. (Dobell 2020; I have heard this story from many sources, including Owen, who taught me at university.)

Writing this monograph reminds me of the optimism shared by most Whitlam-era Australians for a peaceful regional environment and a stronger international order. Under-addressed here are closer relations with India, one of Whitlam's objectives, a relationship now coming into its own at the time of writing. The legacy of post-colonial resentment had to be factored. This too applies to Indonesia. *Konfrontasi* and the killing of hundreds of thousands of Chinese in 1965, which put the country out of contention as an ally in the 1960s. Whitlam did much to build better relations, but memories of East Timor linger today. To his great credit, Whitlam recognised how bitter the colonial experience had been and clearly accounted for it in Australian policy. Today, nothing looks more sensible than a closer Indonesian alliance with Australia, but for various reasons, we do not figure greatly on their radar – unless we buy advanced planes and submarines. It is wonderful, though, to see in 2022 Prime Minister Anthony Albanese and President Joko Widodo strike an apparently warm rapport. But, overall, relations are not close, if business-to-business interactions, the learning of Indonesian in Australian schools, is part of the evidence. As Stephen Fitzgerald lamented, in thinking in a wider context about China recognition 50 years before:

> Starting in the early years of this century, interest in Asia, particularly Southeast Asia and ASEAN, fell into decline. This decline took its lead from the messages and signalling of government, with a not very effective swing back under the Labor governments of Gillard and Rudd. There was a dramatic fall in the numbers studying Asian languages and societies, and a very visible loss of interest in the region by the mainstream media (S. Fitzgerald 2022).

This represents part of the closing of the Australian mind – intellectual, linguistic, cultural, and business – to deeper relations with the various countries to Australia's north.

If, because of my efforts here, further research is stimulated about the Whitlam moment in Australian foreign policy, the writing of this monograph will prove worthwhile.

Finally, I should thank my former Social Studies teacher in Second Form (Year 8) at Marist Brothers' Penshurst, Mr Ford, who was obviously bored with the curriculum. One day he demanded that members of the class nominate whom they supported among the Labor, Liberal, and the Democratic Labor parties. The next week I had to defend my choice in front of 60 students. Whitlam was then my inspiration. In some ways he still is. I had to grow up to realise some of his limitations. In assessing those, I do not write Whitlam off as unforgiveable or deplorable for his mistakes, the current mode of things. I might now be clearer sighted, but once a dewy-eyed Whitlamite, it is hard to lose affection for the good he strove for, no matter the missteps along the way.

BIBLIOGRAPHY

Acheson, D., 1970, *Present at the Creation. My Years in the State Department*, London: Hamish Hamilton.

Adams, D., 1976, "Political Review", *The Australian Quarterly*, Vol. 48, No. 1, March, pp. 115-126.

AFAR, 1975, "Disbandment of ANZUK Force", *Australian Foreign Affairs Record*, Vol. 46, No. 1, January, p. 44.

Australian Jewish News Report [AJN], 1975, "Whitlam Raises Jewish Question in Russian Tour", *Australian Jewish News*, 16 January, p. 1.

Australian Jewish News Report [AJN] Editorial, 1975, "The Election", *Australian Jewish News*, 11 December, p. 2.

Australian Jewish News Report [AJN], 1976, "Labor MLA Disowns Deals with Irakis", *Australian Jewish News*, 4 March, p. 3.

Albinski, H.S., 1977, *Australian External Policy Under Labor. Content, Process and The National Debate*, St. Lucia: University of Queensland Press.

Ball, D., 1980, *A Suitable Piece of Real Estate. American Installations in Australia*, Sydney: Hall & Iremonger.

Ball, W.M., 1945, "Introduction", Evatt, H.V., 1945, *Foreign Policy of Australia. Speeches*, Sydney: Angus & Robertson, pp. v-xii.

Ball, W.M., 1974, "The Foreign Policy of the Whitlam Government", *Australia's Neighbours* [Australian Institute of International Affairs], Fourth Series, No. 90, April-June, pp. 1-4.

Ball, D., & Wilson, H., (eds.), 1991, *Strange Neighbours. The Australia-Indonesia Relationship*, North Sydney: Allen & Unwin.

Bayuni, E., 2018, "Indonesia and Australia: Ties that Rarely Bind", Lindsey, T., & McRae, D., (eds.), 2018, *Strangers Next Door? Indonesia and Australia in the Asian Century*, Oxford: Hart Publishing, pp. 287-304.

Beazley, K.C., 1983, "Federal Labor and the Vietnam Commitment", in Peter King (ed), 1983, *Australia's Vietnam. Australia in the Second Indo-China War*, Sydney: George Allen & Unwin, 36-55.

Beazley, K.C., 2016, "Sovereignty and the U.S. Alliance", in Dean, P.J., Frühling, S. & Taylor, B. (eds.), 2016, *Australia's American Alliance*, Carlton: Melbourne University Press, 203-223.

Beazley, K.E., 2009, *Father of the House. The Memoirs of Kim E. Beazley*, North Fremantle: Fremantle Press.

Bell, C., 1977, *The Diplomacy of Détente. The Kissinger Era*, London: Martin Robertson.

Bell, C., 1988a, "Whitlam and His Fall, 1972-75", in Bell, C., 1988, *Dependent Ally. A Study in Australian Foreign Policy*, Melbourne: Oxford University Press 114-142.

Bell, C., 1988b, "ANZUS in Australia's Foreign and Security Policies", in Jacob Bercovitch (ed.), 1988, *ANZUS in Crisis. Alliance Management in International Affairs*, Macmillan Press, London, 1988, pp. 136-158.

Bilney, G., 2013, "Foreign and Defence Policy", in Bramston, T. (ed.), 2013b, *The Whitlam Legacy*, Leichhardt: The Federation Press, pp. 270-279.

Bongiorno, F, 2022, *Dreamers and Schemers. A Political History of Australia*, Collingwood: La Trobe University Press with Black Inc.

Bramston, T., (ed.), 2013a, *For the True Believers. Great Labor Speeches that Shaped History*, Leichhardt: The Federation Press.

Bramston, T. (ed.), 2013b, *The Whitlam Legacy*, Leichhardt: The Federation Press.

Bramston, T., 2015, "When Rising Star Gough Whitlam Called in on Lyndon Johnson", *The Australian*, 3 January.

Bramston, T., 2022, *Bob Hawke. Demons and Destiny. The Definitive Biography*, Viking.

Bibliography

Brandis, George, 2022, "Hero, Martyr, Victim... But Was Whitlam a Great Man?", *Sydney Morning Herald*, 5 December.

Brennan, F., 2017, "Citizenship and the Common Good" [The Lionel Bowen Memorial Lecture], *Eureka Street* on-line, https://www.eurekastreet.com.au/article/citizenship-and-the-common-good, accessed 22 July 2022.

The Bulletin's *Complete Guide to Labor's Policies*, 1972, Conpress Print, Sydney.

Burns, C., 1974, "That Even Hand Turns Heavy: Whitlam's Style at Fault: Middle-East Policy is Right, But its Execution Confusing", *The Age*, 22 May 1974.

Calwell, A.A., 1965, "Speech on Australia's Commitment of Troops to Vietnam", House of Representatives *Hansard*, 25th Parliament, 1st Session, 4 May, pp. 1101ff.

Cameron, C., 1990, *The Cameron Diaries*, Sydney: Allen & Unwin.

Chen, K.C., 1979, *The Nixon-Chou Shanghai Communiqué*, in Chen, K.C, (ed.), 1979, *China and the Three Worlds: A Foreign Policy Reader*, White Plains, NY: M. E. Sharpe, pp. 127-132.

Clark, C., (ed.), 1973, *Australian Foreign Policy. Towards A Reassessment*, North Melbourne: Cassell Australia.

Clark, C., 1974, "Problems of Australian Foreign Policy, July to December 1973", *Australian Journal of Politics and History*, Vol. 20, No. 1, March, pp. 1-10.

Connor, M., 2016, "The Iraqi Money Scandal, Forty Years On", *Quadrant*, Vol. 50, No. 3, March, pp. 36-45.

Curran, J., 2004, *The Power of Speech. Australian Prime Ministers Defining the National Image*, Carlton: Melbourne University Press.

Curran, J., 2012, "Dear Mr President. What Did Gough Whitlam Say to Upset Richard Nixon", *The Monthly*, August, pp. 41-45.

Curran, J., 2015, *Unholy Fury. Whitlam and Nixon at War*, Carlton: Melbourne University Press.

Curran, J., 2022, *Australia's China Odyssey. From Euphoria to Fear*, Sydney: NewSouth Publishing.

Dean, P.J., Frühling, S. & Taylor, B. (eds.), 2016, *Australia's American Alliance*, Carlton: Melbourne University Press.

Denoon, D., 2012, *A Trial Separation. Australia and the Decolonisation of Papua New Guinea*, Canberra: Australian National University E Press.

Dobell, G., 2020, "Oz Strategists: Owen Harries. Part 1", *The Strategist*, online publication of the Australian Strategic Policy Institute.

Dorling, Philip, 2011, "How Murdoch got His Biggest Scoop. Whitlam, Fraser and the Iraqi Money Affair Made for a Great Story", *Sydney Morning Herald*, 19 November.

Dorling, Philip, 2013, "The Real Word About Whitlam", *Sydney Morning Herald*, 9 April.

Easson, M.B., 2022, "Promise and Influence of Whitlam's Foreign Policy", Prasser, S., & Clune, D., (eds.), 2022, *The Whitlam Era. A Reappraisal of Government, Politics and Policy*, Redland Bay: Connor Court Publishing, pp. 295-331.

Edwards, P., 2016, "Australia's Forgotten Foreign Minister: Don Willesee", *The Strategist*, online publication of the Australian Strategic Policy Institute, 29 July.

Emy, H., Hughes, O., & Mathews, R. (eds.), 1993, *Whitlam Re-Visited. Policy Development, Policies and Outcomes*, Leichhardt: Pluto Press.

Encel, S., 2004, "Jews and the Australian Labor Party", in Levey, G.B., & Mendes, P., (eds.), 2004, *Jews and Australian Politics*, Brighton: Sussex Academic Press, pp. 47-65.

Evans, G. & Grant, B., 1991, *Australia's Foreign Relations in the World of the 1990s*, Carlton: Melbourne University Press.

Evans, G., 1997, "The Labor Tradition: A View from the 1990s", in Lee, D., & Waters, C. (eds.), 1997, *Evatt to Evans. The Labor Tradition in Australian Foreign Policy*, St Leonards: Allen & Unwin (in association with the Department of International Relations, Research School of Pacific and Asian Studies, ANU), pp. 11-22.

Evatt, H.V, 1943, "Problems of the Pacific", *Free World*, Vol. 5, No. 6, June, pp. 490-494.

Bibliography

Evatt, H.V., 1945, *Foreign Policy of Australia. Speeches*, Sydney: Angus & Robertson.

Fitzgerald, J., 2022, *Cadre Country. How China Became the Chinese Communist Party*, Sydney: UNSW Press.

Fitzgerald, R., & Holt, S., 2010, *Alan "the Red Fox" Reid. Pressman Par Excellence*, Sydney: University of NSW Press.

Fitzgerald, S., 1973, "Australia's China Policy", *Australian Foreign Affairs Record*, Vol. 44, No. 3, March, pp. 176-179.

Fitzgerald, S., 2012, *Talking with China. The Australian Labor Party Visit and Peking's Foreign Policy*, Canberra: Australian National University Press.

Fitzgerald, S., 2015, *Comrade Ambassador. Whitlam's Beijing Envoy*, Carlton: Melbourne University Press.

Fitzgerald, S., 2022, "Opening the Australian Mind: 50 Years of Australia-China Relations", *Pearls & Irritations* website, 10 December, https://johnmenadue.com/opening-the-australian-mind-50-years-of-australia-china-relations, accessed 26 January 2023.

Freudenberg, G., 1977, *A Certain Grandeur*, Melbourne: Macmillan.

Freudenberg, G., 1993, "Aspects of Foreign Policy", Emy, H., Hughes, O., & Mathews, R. (eds.), 1993, *Whitlam Re-Visited. Policy Development, Policies and Outcomes*, Leichhardt: Pluto Press, pp. 200-209.

Freudenberg, G, 2006, *A Figure of Speech: A Political Memoir*, Sydney: Wiley.

Fullilove, M., (ed.), 2005, *'Men and Women of Australia'. Our Greatest Speeches*, Sydney: Vintage.

Garnaut, R., 2000, "The First 25 Years of Searching for Development", *Pacific Economic Bulletin*, pp. 29-36, The first 25 years of searching for development (anu.edu.au), accessed 19 August 2022.

Goldsworthy, D., 1974a, "Foreign Policy Review", *The Australian Quarterly*, Vol. 46, No. 1, March, pp. 104-115.

Goldsworthy, D., 1974b, "Foreign Policy Review", *The Australian Quarterly*, Vol. 46, No. 3, September, pp. 104-112.

Griffin, J., Nelson, H., & Firth, S, 1979, *Papua New Guinea. A Political History*, Richmond: Heinemann Educational Australia.

Gyngell, A., 2017, *Fear of Abandonment. Australia in the World Since 1942*, Carlton: La Trobe University Press in association with Blank Inc.

Harries, O., 1973, "Mr Whitlam and Australian Foreign Policy", *Quadrant*, Vol. 17, No. 4, July-August, pp. 55-64.

Harries. O., 1975a, "The Self-Criticism of E.G. Whitlam", *Quadrant*, Vol. 19, No. 5, August, pp. 42-44.

Harries. O., 1975b, "Australia's Foreign Policy Under Whitlam", *Orbis*, Vol. 19, No. 3, Fall, pp. 1090-1101.

Harries, O., 1977, "Australia's Foreign Policy and the Elections of 1972 and 1975", in Penniman, Howard R. (ed.), 1977), *Australia at the Polls. The National Elections of 1975*, Canberra: Australian National University Press for the American Institute for Public Policy Research, pp. 257-275.

Harries, O., 2009, "the False Choice Between Realism and Morality", *The Interpreter*, Sydney: Lowy Institute (online).

Harries, O., & Windybank, S., 2002, "Sue Windybank talks with Owen Harries", Switzer, T., & Windybank, S., (eds.), 2022, *Prudence and Power. The Writings of Owen Harries*, Redland Bay: Connor Court Publishing, pp. 267-280.

Hartcher, P., 2014, "Gough Whitlam: Political Earthquake Reshaped the Landscape", *Sydney Morning Herald*, 21 October 2014.

Hastings, P., 1973, "A Whitlam Doctrine, But No Foreign Policy", *Sydney Morning Herald*, 5 December, p. 6.

Hawke, R.J., 1994, *The Hawke Memoirs*, Port Melbourne: William Heinemann Australia.

Hawker, Geoffrey, 1974, "Political Review", *The Australian Quarterly*, Vol. 46, No. 4, December, pp. 109-114.

Hayden, W.L., 1996, *Hayden. An Autobiography*, Sydney: Angus & Robertson.

Hearder, J., 2016, "'A Precious Vase'. Sir James Plimsoll", Lowe, David, Lee,

David & Bridge, Carl (eds.), 2016, *Australia Goes to Washington. 75 Years of Australian Representation in the United States, 1940-2015*, Canberra: Australian National University Press, pp. 137-160.

Henderson, G., 1990, "I Gough – the Pitfalls of Martyrdom", *Sydney Morning Herald*, 28 August, p. 11.

Hocking, J., 2012, *Gough Whitlam: His Time. The Biography*, Volume II, Carlton: The Miegunyah Press.

Hudson, W.J., 1972, "Foreign Policy Review", *The Australian Quarterly*, Vol. 44, No. 4, December, pp. 110-119.

Hudson, W.J., 1976, "Problems of Australian Foreign Policy, July to December 1975", *Australian Journal of Politics and History*, Vol. 22, No. 1, April, pp. 1-6.

Job, Peter, 2021, *Narrative of Denial. Australia and the Indonesian Violation of East Timor*, Carlton: Melbourne University Press.

Johns, B., 1974, "Whitlam's Off to Visit the Neighbours", *Sydney Morning Herald*, 28 January.

Keating, P.J., 1995, Ryan, Mark (ed.) *Advancing Australia. The Speeches of Paul Keating, Prime Minister*, Sydney: Big Picture Publications.

Keating, P.J., 1996, "Obsession. Australia and the Challenge of Asia", Keating, P.J., 2011, *After Words. The Post-Prime Ministerial Speeches*, Sydney: Allen & Unwin, pp. 157-180.

Keating, P.J., 2011, *After Words. The Post-Prime Ministerial Speeches*, Sydney: Allen & Unwin.

Kelly, P., 2006, "An Australian View: The Outlook for the Relationship", Monfries, J., (ed.), 2006, *Different Societies, Shared Futures. Australia, Indonesia and the Region*, Singapore: Institute of South-East Asian Studies, pp. 34-38.

Kemp, D., 2022, *Consent of the People 1966-2022. Human Dignity Through Freedom and Equality*, Carlton: The Miegunah Press, Melbourne University Publishing.

Kemp, R., & Stanton, M., (eds.), 2004, *Speaking for Australia. Parliamentary Speeches that Shaped Our Nation*, Crows Nest: Allen & Unwin.

Knopfelmacher, F., 1967, "The Consequences of Israel", *Quadrant*, Vol. 11, No.6, November-December, pp. 55-64.

Koh, T., & Li Lin, C. (eds.), 2005, *The Little Red Dot. Reflections by Singapore's Diplomats*, Singapore: World Scientific Publishing.

Kohn, P., 2013, "Hawke Would Have Quit Over Israel", *Australian Jewish News*, 12 April.

Lee, D., & Waters, C., 1997a, "Introduction", Lee, D., & Waters, C. (eds.), 1997, *Evatt to Evans. The Labor Tradition in Australian Foreign Policy*, St Leonards: Allen & Unwin (in association with the Department of International Relations, Research School of Pacific and Asian Studies, ANU), pp. 1-7.

Lee, D., & Waters, C. (eds.), 1997, eds, *Evatt to Evans. The Labor Tradition in Australian Foreign Policy*, St Leonards: Allen & Unwin (in association with the Department of International Relations, Research School of Pacific and Asian Studies, ANU).

Lee, K.Y., 2000, *From Third World to First. The Singapore Story: 1965-2000*, New York: Harper Collins.

Levey, G.B., & Mendes, P., (eds.), 2004, *Jews and Australian Politics*, Brighton: Sussex Academic Press.

Lindsey, T., & McRae, D., (eds.), 2018, *Strangers Next Door? Indonesia and Australia in the Asian Century*, Oxford: Hart Publishing.

Lowe, D., Lee, D., & Bridge, C. (eds.), 2016, *Australia Goes to Washington. 75 Years of Australian Representation in the United States, 1940-2015*, Canberra: Australian National University Press.

MacIntyre, A., 1991, "Australia-Indonesia Relations", Ball, D., & Wilson, H., (eds.), 1991, *Strange Neighbours. The Australia-Indonesia Relationship*, North Sydney: Allen & Unwin, pp. 145-160.

McLaren, J. (ed.), 1972, *Towards a New Australia*, Melbourne: Cheshire for the Victorian Fabian Society.

Memorandum of Conversation [MoC], 1973, between Shah of Iran, Henry A. Kissinger, and Richard Helms, 27 July 1973, Nixon Presidential

Library Documents, https://www.nixonlibrary.gov/sites/default/files/virtuallibrary/documents/jun09/072773_memcon.pdf, accessed 22 January 2023.

Menadue, J., 1999, *Things You Learn Along the Way*, Melbourne: David Lovell Publishing.

Menadue, J., 2020, "Talk with Friendlyjordies", 12 August, https://johnmenadue.com/john-menadue-talks-with-friendlyjordies/

Mendes, P, 2023, How Did the Australian Jewish Left Respond to the First Wave of Pro-Palestinian Activism from 1967-75", *Australian Jewish Historical Society Journal*, forthcoming.

Miller, J.D.B., 1973, "Problems of Australian Foreign Policy, July to December 1972", *Australian Journal of Politics and History*, Vol. 19, No. 1, March, pp. 1-10.

Miller, J.D.B., 1975, "Problems of Australian Foreign Policy, January to June 1975", *Australian Journal of Politics and History*, Vol. 21, No. 3, December, pp. 1-10.

Mitchell, S., 2006, *Margaret Whitlam. A Biography*, Milsons Point: Random House Australia.

Monfries, J., (ed.), 2006, *Different Societies, Shared Futures. Australia, Indonesia and the Region*, Singapore: Institute of South-East Asian Studies.

Morrison, W.L., 2013, "Papua New Guinea: A Quiet Achievement", in Bramston, T. (ed.), 2013b, *The Whitlam Legacy*, Leichhardt: The Federation Press, pp. 349-356.

Mullins, P., 2018, *Tiberius with a Telephone. The Life and Stories of William McMahon*, Melbourne: Scribe.

Murphy, D.J., 1973, "Problems of Australian Foreign Policy, January to June 1973", *Australian Journal of Politics and History*, Vol. 19, No. 3, December, pp. 331-342.

Murphy, J., 2016, *Evatt. A Life*, Sydney. New South.

NYT, Report, Whitlam and Ford Confer", *New York Times*, 5 October 1974, p. 29.

Oakes, L., 1976, *Crash or Crash Through. The Unmaking of a Prime Minister*, Richmond: Drummond.

O'Neill, R.J., 1972, "Problems of Australian Foreign Policy, July to December 1971", *Australian Journal of Politics and History*, Vol. 18, No. 1, March, pp. 1-17.

Oliver, B., 2010, "Willesee, Donald Robert (1916-2003). Senator for Western Australia, 1950-1975 (Australian Labor Party)", *The Biographical Dictionary of the Australian Senate*, 2010, Vol. 3, 1962-1983, Sydney: University of New South Wales Press Ltd, pp. 478-484.

Palfreeman, A.C., 1972, "Foreign Policy Review", *The Australian Quarterly*, Vol. 44, No. 2, June, pp. 112-121.

Paul, J.B., 1973a, "Political Review", *The Australian Quarterly*, Vol. 45, No. 3, September, pp. 104-115.

Paul, J.B., 1973b, "Political Review", *The Australian Quarterly*, Vol. 45, No. 4, December 1973, pp. 114-127.

Peacock, A.S., 1974, "Mr Whitlam's Foreign Policy", *Sydney Morning Herald*, 14 October, p. 7.

Pemberton, G., 1997, "Whitlam and the Labor Tradition", in Lee, D., & Waters, C. (eds.), 1997, *Evatt to Evans. The Labor Tradition in Australian Foreign Policy*, St Leonards: Allen & Unwin (in association with the Department of International Relations, Research School of Pacific and Asian Studies, ANU), pp. 131-162.

Penniman, Howard R. (ed.), 1977, *Australia at the Polls. The National Elections of 1975*, Canberra: Australian National University Press for the American Institute for Public Policy Research.

Pettman, R., 1974, "Problems of Australian Foreign Policy, January to June 1974", *Australian Journal of Politics and History*, Vol. 20, No. 3, December, pp. 299-311.

Prasser, S., & Clune, D., (eds.), 2022, *The Whitlam Era. A Reappraisal of Government, Politics and Policy*, Redland Bay: Connor Court Publishing.

Reid, A., 1976, *The Whitlam Venture*, Melbourne: Hill of Content.

Reich, Chanan, 2010, "From 'Endemically Pro-Israel' to Unsympathetic:

Australia's Middle East Policy, 1967–1972", *Australian Journal of Politics and History*, Vol. 56, Issue 4, December, pp. 574-591.

Rudd, K., 2008, "Kevin Rudd speaks to Peking University: A Conversation With China's Youth on The Future", Kevin Rudd speaks to Peking University: A Conversation With China's Youth on The Future — Kevin Rudd, accessed 30 January 2023.

Rudd, K, 2018, *The PM Years*, Sydney: Pan Macmillan Australia.

Rudd, K., 2022, *The Avoidable War. The Dangers of a Catastrophic Conflict Between the US and Xi Jinping's China*, New York: PublicAffairs, Hachette Book Group.

Rutland, S.D., 2012, "Whitlam's Shifts in Foreign Policy: Israel and Soviet Jewry", *Australian Journal of Jewish Studies*, Vol. 26, pp. 36-69.

Rutland, S.D., 2014, "Australia and the Struggle for Soviet Jewry: 1961-1972", *Australian Journal of Politics and History*, Vol. 60, No. 2, pp. 194-213.

Rutland, S.D., 2021, *Lone Voice. The Wars of Isi Leibler*, Melbourne: Hybrid Publishers.

St. J. Barclay, G., 1975, "Problems of Australian Foreign Policy, July to December 1974", *Australian Journal of Politics and History*, Vol. 21, No. 1, April, pp. 1-10.

Santamaria, B.A., 1973, "The First Six Months: 'The Style is Less of Independence than of Precipitance'", *Current Affairs Bulletin*, Vol. 50, No. 2, July, pp. 8-11.

Santamaria, B.A., 1974, "We've Moved into the Orbit of Communism", *Focus* (organ of the Democratic Labor Party in NSW), September, pp. 9-12.

Sexton, M, 2005, *The Great Crash. The Short Life and Sudden Death of the Whitlam Government*, Carlton North: Scribe Publications.

Sirox Kari, S., 2005, "The Origin and Setting of the National Goals and Directive Principles in the Process of Writing the Constitution of Papua New Guinea", PhD Thesis, Queensland University of Technology.

SMH, 1960, "Whitlam Attacks Foreign Policy", *Sydney Morning Herald*, 21 June, p. 5.

SMH, 1964, "Plea for Informed Public", *Sydney Morning Herald*, 28 January.

SMH, 1970, "Foreign Policy in Ruins – Whitlam", *Sydney Morning Herald*, 16 September, p. 12.

SMH, 1972, "What the election is about... Foreign policy", *Sydney Morning Herald*, 1 November, p. 6.

SMH, 1987, "Whitlam's Men Look Back on Summer Storm", *Sydney Morning Herald*, 19 December, p. 12.

Standish, B., 1976, "Papua New Guinea Review", *The Australian Quarterly*, Vol. 48, No. 2, June, pp. 106-119.

Stockwin, J.A.A., 1972, "Problems of Australian Foreign Policy, January to June 1972", *Australian Journal of Politics and History*, Vol. 18, No. 3, December, pp. 331-343.

Stone, J., 1943, *The Atlantic Charter. New Worlds for Old*, Sydney: Angus and Robertson.

Suter, K.D., 1975, "The Australian Government's Policy of Recognition and Diplomatic Relations", *The Australian Quarterly*, Vol. 47, No. 3, September, pp. 67-79.

Switzer, T., & Windybank, S., (eds.), 2022, *Prudence and Power. The Writings of Owen Harries*, Redland Bay: Connor Court Publishing.

Tange, A., 2008, *Defence Policy Making. A Close-Up View, 1950-1980. A Personal Memoir*, Edwards, P. (ed.), Strategic and Defence Studies Centre, Canberra Papers on Strategy and Defence No. 169, Canberra: ANU E Press.

Van der Kroef, J.M., 1970, *Australian Security Policies and Problems*, New York: National Strategy Information Centre.

Viviani, N., 1984, *The Long Journey: Vietnamese Migration and Settlement in Australia*, Carlton: Melbourne University Press.

Viviani, N., 1997, "The Whitlam Government's Policy Towards Asia", Lee, D., & Waters, C. (eds.), 1997, *Evatt to Evans. The Labor Tradition in Australian Foreign Policy*, St Leonards: Allen & Unwin (in association with the Department of International Relations, Research School of Pacific and Asian Studies, ANU), pp. 99-109.

Bibliography

Wallace, C., 2023, *Political Lives. Australian Prime Ministers and Their Biographers*, Sydney: UNSW Press.

Walsh, J.R. & Munster, G.J. (eds.), 1980, *Documents on Australian Defence and Foreign Policy 1968-1975*, Hong Kong.

Walsh, J.R. & Munster, G.J., 1982, *Secrets of State. A Detailed Assessment of the Book They Banned*, Sydney: Walsh & Munster.

Watson, B.J., 2021, *Forgotten Island: Australia, Realism and the Timor Crisis*, Australian Scholarly Publishing.

White, H., 2018, "The Jakarta Switch", *Australian Foreign Affairs*, Issue 3, July, pp. 7-30.

White, H., 2019, "A Very Unreassuring Bombshell: Richard Nixon and the Guam Doctrine, July 1969", *The Strategist*, publication of the Australian Strategic Policy Institute, 25 July, A very unreassuring bombshell: Richard Nixon and the Guam doctrine, July 1969 | The Strategist (aspistrategist.org.au), accessed 5 August 2022.

Whitlam, E.G., 1972, "Australia and Her Region", McLaren, J. (ed.), 1972, *Towards a New Australia*, Melbourne: Cheshire for the Victorian Fabian Society, pp.1-19.

Whitlam, E.G., 1973a, "Foreword", Clark, C., (ed.), 1973, *Australian Foreign Policy. Towards A Reassessment*, North Melbourne: Cassell Australia, pp. vii-viii.

Whitlam, E.G., 1973b, "Opening Address to Conference", in Gordon McCarthy (ed.), 1973, *Foreign Policy for Australia. Choices for the Seventies*, Melbourne: Angus and Robertson for the Australian Institute of Political Science, pp. 1-7.

Whitlam, E.G., 1973c, "Australia's Foreign Policy" [reprint of a statement delivered to the House of Representatives, 24 May], *Australian Foreign Affairs Record*, Vol. 44, No. 5, May 1973, pp. 335-344. (Also at *Hansard*, House of Representatives, 28th Parliament, 1st Session, 24 May, pp. 2643-2652.)

Whitlam, E.G., 1973d, *Australia's Foreign Policy: New Directions, New Definitions*, Twenty-Fourth Roy Milne Memorial Lecture, Brisbane, 30 November,

Australian Institute of International Affairs, Ramsay, Ware Publishing.

Whitlam, E.G., 1975a, "The Prime Minister Addresses Parliament after his Mission to Europe", *Australian Foreign Affairs Record*, Vol. 46, No. 2, February, pp. 60-69. (Also at *Hansard*, House of Representatives, 29th Parliament, 1st Session, 11 February, pp. 61-66.)

Whitlam, E.G., 1975b, "Australia and International Law" (speech delivered to a seminar in Canberra on 'Public International Law'), *Australian Foreign Affairs Record*, Vol. 46, No. 8, August, pp. 448-450.

Whitlam, E.G., 1981, *A Pacific Community*, Cambridge: Harvard University Press.

Whitlam, E.G., 1985, *The Whitlam Government 1872-1975*, Ringwood: Viking.

Willesee, D., 1975, "Australia and the Non-Aligned Movement", *Australian Foreign Affairs Record*, Vol. 46, No. 8, August, p. 446.

Wong, P., 2022, "Whitlam Oration", 13 November, Whitlam Oration Australian Minister for Foreign Affairs (foreignminister.gov.au), accessed 26 January 2023.

Woodard, G., 2018, "Australia's China Policy of Strategic Ambiguity: Navigating Between Big Fish", *Australian Journal of International Affairs*, Vol. 72, No. 2, pp. 163-178.

Woolcott, R., 2003, *The Hot Seat. Reflections on Diplomacy from Stalin's Death to the Bali Bombings*, Sydney: Harper Collins.

Woolcott, R., 2018, "A Rising Regional Neighbour of Increasing Importance", Lindsey, T., & McRae, D., (eds.), 2018, *Strangers Next Door? Indonesia and Australia in the Asian Century*, Oxford: Hart Publishing, pp. 11-17.

Index

"All the Way with LBJ", 39
Acheson, Dean, 9, 22, 89, 95
Agnew, Spiro, 43
Albanese, Anthony, 92
Albinski, Henry, 24, 69, 95
Alice Springs, 49, 50
Al-Tikriti, Ghafil Jassim, 80
Angola, 62
ANZUK, 95
ANZUS, 8, 25, 36, 96
apartheid, 15, 16, 73
Arafat, Yasser, 80
ASEAN, 24, 92
Atlantic Charter, 14, 15, 106
Australian Council of Trade Unions (ACTU), 70, 76
Australian Jewish News, 70, 75, 95, 102
Australian nationalism, 11, 13, 14, 44
Australian Secret Intelligence Service (ASIS), 46
Australian Signals Directorate, 46
AXIS alliance, 15
Baghdad Bill. *See* Hartley, Bill
Bahamas, 13
Balibo, 64
Ball, Des, 50
Ball, W. Macmahon, 83
Baltic States, 56, 66, 87
Barbados, 13

Barnard, Lance, 49, 50, 86
Barnes, C.E. "Ceb", 22
Barwick, Garfield, 17
Bases, 45
Beazley, Kim C., 45, 46, 58, 90
Beazley, Kim E., 45, 47, 65, 81, 87
Bell, Coral, 18, 47, 49
Berinson, Joe, 75
Biafra, 13
Bilney, Gordon, 10, 57
Bowen, Lionel, 67, 81, 97
Bramston, Troy, 37, 39, 58, 72, 96, 103
Brandis, George, 88, 97
Brennan, Fr. Frank, 67, 97
Browning, Michaela, 90
Burns, Creighton, 76
Bush, George H.W., 43
Calwell, Arthur, 17, 37, 45, 46, 58
Cameron, Clyde, 61, 97
Canada, 28
caravanserai, 54
Carnation Revolution, 62
Caro, Robert A., 39, 40
Casey, Richard, 51, 83
Cass, Moss, 75
Chen, King C., 28, 97
Chiang Kai-shek, 29
Chifley, Ben, 15

Child, Joan, 75
Chile, 13, 17
China. *See* People's Republic of China (PRC)
Chinese Communist Party (CCP), 86
Churchill, Winston, 14
Clark, Claire, 22, 28, 44
Clune, David, 90, 98, 101
Cohen, Barry, 75
Cold War, 23, 29, 65, 91
Convention on the Political Rights of Women, 16
Coombe, David, 79
Costello, Michael, 90
Cuba, 62
Curran, James, 14, 29, 43, 44, 49, 97
Cyclone Tracy, 54, 55, 56
Defence Signals Division, 46
Deng Xiaoping, 29
Denoon, Donald, 33, 98
détente, 66
Diego Garcia, 24, 25
Dobell, Graeme, 91
Dorling, Philip, 70, 74, 80
Dunstan, Don, 75
Dutch West Indies, 62
Easson, Mary, 3
Easson, Michael, 44, 98
Easson, Shane, 90
East Germany, 13
East Timor, 8, 25, 61, 62, 63, 64, 65, 87, 91
Edwards, Peter, 88
Ehrlichman, John D., 44

Einfeld, Syd, 74, 75
Encel, Sol, 71
Equal Remuneration Convention, 16
Evans, Gareth, 7, 14
Evatt, Herbert Vere, 15
Faulkner, John, 67
Fischer, Henry, 80
Fitzgerald, John, 87
Fitzgerald, Stephen, 13, 28, 29, 31, 92
Five Power Defence Arrangements FPDA, 19
Five Power Defence Arrangements Integrated Area Defence System, 19
Ford, Barry, 92
Ford, Gerald, 41, 42, 64
Formosa, 31
Fraser, Malcolm, 17, 22, 64
Fretilin, 63
Freudenberg, Graham, 29, 37, 46, 59, 60, 61, 54, 66, 77, 99
Fullilove, Michael, 58
Garnaut, Ross, 34, 99
Gillard, Julia, 92
Golan Heights, 72, 77
Goldsworthy, David, 48, 50, 82, 85
Grace, Damian, 90
Graham, Rev. Billy, 39
Grant, Bruce, 7
Griffin, James, 34
Guam doctrine, 21
Guatemala, 13
Guinea-Bissau, 13
Guise, Sir John, 34
Guyana, 13

Index

Gyngell, Allan, 64
Haiphong, 42
Halderman, Harry R. 44
Hanoi, 42
Harding, Catherine, 90
Harries, Owen, 25, 82, 91
Hartcher, Peter, 32
Hartley, Bill, 79, 80
Hastings, Peter, 22
Hawke, RJL "Bob", 35, 38, 39
Hayden, William "Bill", 81
Hearder, Jeremy, 43
Helms, Richard, 24
Henderson, Gerard, 81
Hocking, Jenny, 63, 64, 79
Holding, Clyde, 75
Holt, Harold, 36, 37, 45
Holy See, 13
Howard, John, 84
Hu Yaobang, 86
Hudson, William J., 83
Hussein, Saddam, 74, 80
India, 16, 24, 91
Indian Ocean, 24, 45, 59
Indonesia, 16, 17, 21, 25, 34, 51, 52, 53, 59, 62, 63, 64, 65, 83, 88, 92
International Convention on the Elimination of All Forms of Racial Discrimination, 16
International Court of Justice, 12
International Labour Organization (ILO), 15, 76
International Women's Conference, 73, 76
Iran, 24

Iraq, 13
Iraqi Ba'ath Socialist Party, 8, 74, 79, 81
Irian Jaya, 17, 62, 65
Isolationism, 44, 58
Israeli Labour Party, 75
Jamaica, 13
Japan, 21, 22, 30, 59
Johnson, Lyndon Baines, 36, 37, 38, 39, 40
Joint Facilities, 46, 47
Keating, Paul, 24
Kelly, Paul, 52, 53
Kemp, David, 58, 73
Kissinger, Henry, 24, 27, 28, 29, 41, 42, 43, 48, 64, 85
Klugman, Richard "Dick", 75
Knopfelmacher, Frank, 71, 72
Koh, Tommy, 90
Kohn, Peter, 71
Konfrontasi, 20, 91
Kosygin, Alexei, 67, 68, 74
Labor Council of NSW (now called Unions NSW), 81
Labor Left, 86
Lebanon, The, 69, 76
Lee Kuan Yew, 60
MacIntyre, Andrew, 53
Malaysia, 17, 19, 20
Mao Tse-tung, 29, 30, 31, 91
McClelland, James Robert "Jim", 81
McMahon, William, 27, 28, 33, 58, 91
Meir, Golda, 70
Menadue, John, 46, 55, 56, 60, 64
Mendes, Philip, 68, 71, 75, 90

Menzies, Sir Robert, 46, 57
Middle East, 56, 68, 69, 70, 71, 72, 77, 80, 90
Mitchell, Susan, 32
Morrison, Scott, 56
Morrison, WL "Bill", 18, 34
Mozambique, 62
Mullins, Patrick, 28
Munster, George, 3163
Murphy, Denis J., 21, 22
Murphy, John, 15
NARA Agreement, 22
Nessen, Ron, 41
Nicholson, Peter, 32
Nixon, Richard M., 28, 40
Non-Aligned Movement, 20, 24, 45
North Korea, 13
North Vietnam, 13
Nurrungar, 47, 49, 50
Oakes, Laurie, 80, 87, 104
occupied territories, 69
Oliver, Bobbie, 12, 51, 61, 64, 66
OPEC, 71
Operation Carlotta, 62
Palestine Liberation Organisation (PLO), 76, 80
Palfreeman, A.C. "Tony", 22, 91
Papua New Guinea (PNG), 8, 11, 17, 25, 33, 34
Patolichev, Nikolai, 66
Patterson, Rex, 27
Paul, J.B. "John", 7, 54
Peacock, Andrew, 24, 43, 66, 84, 104
Peoples' Republic of China (PRC), 12, 13, 16, 17, 19, 21, 27

Philhellene, 54
Pine Gap, 47, 49, 50, 86
Plimsoll, James, 43, 44, 112
Pragmatism, 11, 85
Prasser, Scott, 90, 104
prima donna assoluta, 44, 87
Rabin, Yitzhak, 69
Renouf, Alan, 66, 68
Rhodesia, 13
Riordan, Joe, 75
Roosevelt, Franklin Delano, 13, 14
Rothman, Stephen, 90
Royal Australian Air Force, 14, 50
Royal Malaysian Air Force, 19
Rudd, Kevin, 86, 87, 92, 105
Rural Electrification Administration (REA), 37, 38
Rutland, Suzanne, 68, 72, 73, 74, 75, 76, 80, 90
Saigon, 58, 60
Saudi Arabia, 13
Scarf, Reuben F., 80
Schlesinger, James R., 50
SEATO, 18
Shanghai Communiqué, 28
Shoah, The, 73
Singapore, 19
Sirox Kari, Sam, 33
Six Day war, 71
Snedden, Billy, 54, 56
Socialist Left, 72, 79
Soeharto, President, 52, 53, 63, 65, 112
Somare, Michael, 35

Index

South Africa, 16, 97
South Pacific Forum, 13, 22
South Vietnam, 42, 58, 60, 61, 83
Spigelman, James "Jim", 44, 73
Standish, Bill, 33
Stone, Julius, 15
Strategic Arms Limitation Talks, 84
Sudan, 13
Suez Canal, 75
Suter, Keith, 13, 66
Switzer, Tom, 25, 82, 90, 100
Taiwan, 19, 28, 29, 31
Tanaka, Kakuei, 44
Tange, Arthur, 49, 106
Tel Aviv, 69
Terrill, Ross, 43
Tientsin, 32
Trinidad and Tobago, 13
Trips, 8, 25, 54, 55
UNESCO, 76
Union of Soviet Socialist Republics (USSR), 13, 24, 43, 66
United Nations (UN), 12, 16, 23, 58
Universal Declaration of Human Rights, 16
University of NSW ALP Club, 81
US Alliance, 11, 17, 45, 57, 86
van der Kroef, Justus M, 19, 106
Venezuela, 13
Victorian Labor Unity, 69
Vietnam, 12, 17, 21, 25, 37, 40
Vietnamese Balts, 61
Vietnamese refugees, 8, 61, 87
Vietnamisation, 22

Viviani, Nancy, 8, 11, 12, 13, 15, 17, 23, 61, 65, 106
Wallace, Christine "Chris", 37
Waller, Keith, 30
Walsh, J. Richard, 63
Watson, Bruce J., 64, 66, 65, 107
West Bank, 71, 77
West New Guinea (Irian Jaya), 17, 62, 65
Wheeldon, John, 31, 81
White Australia policy, 12, 17
Whitlam, Margaret, 28, 32, 103
Whitlamism, 8, 10, 11, 13, 15, 17, 18, 19, 21, 23, 25, 88, 89
Widodo, Joko, 92
Wikileaks, 70
Wilenski, Peter, 43, 44, 73
Willesee, Don, 7, 12, 20, 26, 50, 61, 64, 66, 85, 87, 88, 98, 104, 108
Windybank, Susan, 25, 82, 90, 100, 106
Wong, Penny, 33
Woodard, Garry, 28
Woolcott, Richard "Dick", 10, 23, 51, 52, 63, 108
Xi, Jinping, 87
Yehya, Farouk Abdulla, 80
Yom Kippur War, 50, 71, 72, 74, 75, 77
Zhao Ziyang, 86
zhengyou, 86
Zhongnanhai, 30
Zhou Enlai, 27, 30
Zionism, 73, 76

www.ingramcontent.com/pod-product-compliance
Ingram Content Group UK Ltd.
Pitfield, Milton Keynes, MK11 3LW, UK
UKHW021326180426
11947UKWH00017B/1460